HARD CORPS

HARD CORPS

FROM GANGSTER TO MARINE HERO

Marco Martinez

THREE RIVERS PRESS
NEW YORK

Out of respect for the privacy of individuals mentioned in Chapter 1,
some names have been changed.

Originally published in hardcover in the United States by Crown Forum,
an imprint of the Crown Publishing Group, a division of
Random House, Inc., New York, in 2007.

Library of Congress Cataloging-in-Publication Data
Martinez, Marco, 1981–
Hard Corps : from gangster to Marine hero / Marco Martinez.—
1st ed.
1. Martinez, Marco, 1981– 2. United States. Marine Corps—Biography.
3. Marines—United States—Biography. 4. Iraq War, 2003– I. Title.
VE25.M37A3 2007
956.7044'373092—dc22
[B] 2007023011

ISBN 978-0-307-38305-1

Printed in the United States of America

Design by Lauren Dong

10 9 8 7 6 5 4 3 2 1

First Paperback Edition

This book is dedicated in loving memory of my father,
Marco Martinez Sr.
Dad, I'm sorry that you had to go so soon, I know you
watch over me every day.
I hope you can read this from way up there.

This book is also for all the Marines, Sailors, Soldiers, and Airmen who have shed blood, sweat, and tears in the War on Terror. And to all the brave parents and family members who see their loved ones off to war, God bless. To all Marines, past, present, and future GET SOME!!!

Contents

It's better to die on your feet
than to live on your knees.

—EMILIANO ZAPATA

OFFICIAL NAVY CROSS CITATION

―――――

The President of the United States

Takes Pleasure in Presenting

The Navy Cross

to

MARCO MARTINEZ

UNITED STATES MARINE CORPS

―――――

For Services as Set Forth in the Following:

For extraordinary heroism while serving as First Fire Team Leader, 2nd Squad, 1st Platoon, Company G, 2nd Battalion, 5th Marines, 1st Marine Division, I Marine Expeditionary Force in support of Operation IRAQI FREEDOM on 12 April 2003. Responding to a call to reinforce his Platoon that was ambushed, Corporal Martinez effectively deployed his team under fire in supporting positions for a squad assault. After his squad leader was wounded, he took control and led the assault through a tree line where the ambush originated. As his squad advanced to secure successive enemy positions, it received sustained small arms fire from a nearby building. Enduring intense enemy fire and without regard for his own personal safety,

Corporal Martinez launched a captured enemy rocket propelled grenade into the building temporarily silencing the enemy and allowing a wounded Marine to be evacuated and receive medical treatment. After receiving additional fire, he single-handedly assaulted the building and killed four enemy soldiers with a grenade and his rifle. By his outstanding display of decisive leadership, unlimited courage in the face of heavy enemy fire, and utmost devotion to duty, Corporal Martinez reflected great credit upon himself and upheld the highest traditions of the Marine Corps and the United States Naval Service.

WARNING:

If profanity offends you, consider yourself warned.
A Marine memoir without profanity is like a rifle
without ammo.
This book is locked and loaded.

Prologue

A Step Forward, a Look Back

FOR THE FIRST seventeen years of my life, I was a shithead.

That's the term some Marines use to describe a guy who lacks discipline, focus, and training. But I wasn't just any shithead. I was a *grade-A* shithead, a gangbanging, trash-talking thug. I was the kind of loser who today I—and probably you—can't stand. From stealing cars to beating the hell out of guys just because I could, to "tagging," to sporting a gang tattoo, you name it and I probably did it.

I'm not proud of any of this, mind you. Not in the least. I was ungrateful, disrespectful, and devoid of purpose or virtue. The way I see it, I was a waste of perfectly good oxygen that somebody who was doing good in the world could have used.

And that's why on May 3, 2004, standing at attention, with Secretary of the Navy Gordon England smiling at me as he pinned the Navy Cross to my chest, I felt embarrassed and unworthy. Just behind Secretary Gordon stood Lieutenant Colonel O'Donohue and Sergeant Major Davis. My beaming mother was in the crowd just behind them. Media were all around.

I wondered *What if all these people knew what a punk-ass idiot I was? My Marine brothers deserve this honor, not me.*

At any moment I expected someone to tap Secretary Gordon on the shoulder and tell him that they had the wrong guy—that the United States Marine Corps made a mistake and couldn't dare award the second-highest honor a Marine can receive, second only to the Medal of Honor, to a former thug like me. But it never happened. The ceremony just kept going.

They read the Navy Cross citation to the crowd. The words took me back to April 12, 2003. That was the day on which I fought my way through an ambush sprung by the Fedayeen Saddam and Special Republican Guard that ended in a bloody, house-to-house, close-quarter battle that became known as the Battle of the Bridge. That was also the day on which a platoon-sized force of kick-ass Marines (about fifty people) beat the hell out of a company-sized group of about 200 terrorists. My brother grunts were epic that day. They fought brilliantly. But not everyone would make it through unscathed. And that's something that none of us will ever forget.

I'm humbled beyond words to have been awarded the Navy Cross and become a tiny asterisk in the long, glorious history of our beloved Corps. But the truth is that all my brothers deserved medals as much as—if not more than—some kid born in El Paso, Texas, and raised in Albuquerque, New Mexico. The fact that I was on terminal leave by the time of the ceremony meant that I never got to wear my Navy Cross in uniform. Sometimes I think that was divine justice.

Following the ceremony and media interviews, I found my mother and we headed back to her hotel. Driving through San Mateo, I looked at the barracks and the Regimental Headquarters. This was going to be the last time I would see the place. I passed through the Cristianitos Gate, the invisible wall separating the Marine world from the civilian world. My buddies and I had crossed through that gate many a Sunday morning after nights spent boozing in Los Angeles. But that was now ending. Never again would we feel the rush of air that fills a CH-46 at 13,000 feet or hold the rifles that we killed America's enemies with. Some say that your first enlistment is your best. I think that must be true, because I can't see how it could have been any better. Today, my college classmates or other people my age will sometimes ask how I could "waste" the best years of my life grinding it out as a grunt. "Well," I ask them, "how did you do what *you* did? What friends—not your relatives, but your friends—do you have who you *know* would die for you?"

They rarely have an answer.

Minutes after the Navy Cross ceremony, other memories started kicking inside me. Scenes and mental snapshots flashed through my mind: the sadness in my father's eyes when he realized I'd gone astray; my gang tattoo that almost prevented me from making it through boot camp; boot camp itself, which was *far* more intense than any gang initiation; my drill instructor (DI), who was fiercer than any gangbanger could hope to be; the Iraqi man I met whose tongue had been chopped off because he spoke against Saddam's regime; the eerie feeling that hung over the mass graves we guarded in Iraq; and the book of human experiment pictures that I and a few others discovered in Iraq, images I still can't shake out of my head. But mostly the ceremony made me think about how grateful I was to the men I served and fought with and to those who shaped us, like First Sergeant Bell and Staff Sergeant Waters.

I don't have some lame, "victim" excuse for why I chose to be a thug before I joined the Corps. And even if I did, I hate it when people don't take ownership of their own dirt. So let me just say that being a dumbass is all on me. My parents weren't perfect, but my dad and my beautiful mother loved and raised me and my triplet sisters the right way, with strong values of faith and family. Those values sustain me, and the older I get the stronger and more relevant those values seem to be. It's just the damn cursing I can't seem to kick. (If you're a Marine, I know you feel me.)

When my father came to America, he earned his citizenship while proudly serving as an Army Ranger. For him, loving the military and loving America were one and the same. My father was a giant in my eyes and still is. But I rebelled anyhow. I think his distinguished military service and the pride and respect he commanded intimidated me to the point of rebellion. Back then, my subconscious thinking was, *If you never attempt to live up to his achievements, you'll never fail.* And failure has always been my greatest fear.

So, while I'm not proud of my past, it's an important part of my story. Maybe that ruins the image others might want to superimpose on "the first Hispanic-American since Vietnam to be awarded the Navy Cross, second only to the Medal of Honor," as the press releases read. But I think most Marines will appreciate this approach. The Marines I know don't have a whole lot of patience for bullshit. In fact, a healthy hatred of bullshit is hardwired into us; it's part of our training. Come to think of it, we Marines hate a lot of things: We hate whiny "boots" (new Marines), we hate antimilitary liberals, we hate those patchouli-smelling hippies who denied our Vietnam brothers the honor they were and are due (*damn* we hate those sons of bitches!), we hate pricks like Senator John "I married rich" Kerry who think their Ivy League diplomas somehow make them better than all us military dum-dums who didn't study hard enough and got "stuck in Iraq" (what an arrogant ass that guy is), we hate those people you always see on TV ranting against the very military that protects their First Amendment rights with guns and guts, and we hate that fuckhead Anthony Swofford who wrote that stupid-ass book *Jarhead* that got turned into a stupid-ass movie (I read the book in Iraq and then promptly burned it so that some poor grunt would not have to suffer through that whiny drivel).

You might think this is a lot of hatred to lug around.

Maybe so. But you have to understand Marine Infantry psychology. Grunts are, at base, masochists. We love the crap that no one in his right mind would enjoy. And here's my theory: I think many of us want the abuse. As a fellow Navy Cross recipient, First Sergeant Justin LeHew—a hero if ever there was one—put it, "A guy joins the Corps for one of two reasons: either he has something to prove to someone else, or he has something to prove to himself." I think he's exactly right.

It doesn't matter what state a guy comes from, how much money his family has, what color his skin is, or what his religion is. At our core, Marines are the same. When we say we are brothers, we mean it. No one dies for an "acquaintance." But a brother . . . that's different.

Contrary to the views of guys like Swofford who trash the Corps, I have to say that the United States Marine Corps (USMC) didn't *ruin* my life. It *saved* my life. And I'll forever be grateful for the USMC and all it represents to each of us who've been shaped and steeled by it. If antimilitary bitches want to say that makes me a "brainwashed pawn," then let them. I know otherwise. If they want to say that the military breeds violence, I disagree. And I should know. Sometimes it takes having used violence for both evil as well as good to know that there's a profound moral difference between the two.

Violence isn't senseless. Senseless violence is senseless.

TODAY WHEN I walk down the street with my girlfriend, sometimes I'll see an old veteran wearing his navy blue ship hat or an old-timer proudly wearing his pins. "Look at that guy," I'll tell her. "He was on the *USS* . . . Do you know the hell that guy lived through?" And then the old warrior's eyes will lock on mine and mine on his. Then the slow-moving Salt Dog will grin and give me one of those quick head nods guys give each other—that fast snap of the neck that says, *"I remember, son. I was there, too. I was you, and one day, you'll be me."*

I felt a similar sense of camaraderie when we came home from Iraq and landed in Bangor, Maine, where the legendary "troop greeters" welcomed us home. God bless those people. These wonderful silver-haired people came up to us, slow and sweet, some of them now in their eighties, to make us feel welcome. Almost all of the men had fought in past wars, and the amazing women who loved and supported them while they were overseas whipping the world are still right by their side, all these years later.

I remember one Vietnam veteran in particular. He just wrapped his arms around me and hugged me like I was his son.

"Never be ashamed of your service," he said.

"I can't be ashamed, sir," I said. "Because we did it for America."

His eyes watered and he handed me a cell phone. "Call your folks, son. I'm sure they are worried about you." I took the phone from his outstretched hand and looked around. Many of my brother Marines were sharing similar experiences with the old patriotic men and women who still believed in America and her defenders. I paid careful attention to the Vietnam vets. They took a great deal of pride in their appreciation of us. They radiated joy. And in their kindness I sensed they felt they were giving us the things they yearned for but never received—respect and an honorable homecoming. And that's about when chills like spiders started crawling up my spine. If you served, you know exactly what I mean.

Rusty old Marines, sailors, soldiers, and airmen will tell you the same thing: The military taught us how to be men and how special it is to be Americans. That's why every Marine you will ever meet—young or old, black, white, or brown—burns with love for the Marine brotherhood. Deep down, most of us are hardcore in our devotion to the Corps. We are Hard Corps.

1

Sixteen with a Bullet

The 9 mm Smith & Wesson balanced on my right thigh had its grip wrapped in white medical tape. It was a big son of a bitch, and it had been fired numerous times before. An engraving tool had been used to scratch and grind the trigger. This, along with the tape, would make lifting fingerprints all but impossible. Over the last two years, I'd held and fired numerous weapons. When TEC-9s were cool, we would drive out to New Mexico deserts and shoot shit up. But this was something different. The 9 mm resting on my leg wasn't going to be used for target practice.

"I wish this pussy-ass muthafucka would hurry up and get home," Damien said as he looked at the house three doors down the street. "I'm ready to do this."

We were both ready to do this. We'd cinched knots in the rags wrapped around our heads and tucked them up under our hats so they could be quickly yanked down to cover our faces, like a train robber would in a western. My rag was brown. Damien's was black. That day I wore stereotypical 1990s-style Hispanic gangster gear, complete with Ben Davis threads, Mad Dogg sunglasses with "100% Chicano" emblazoned on the sides, and a black baseball cap with RAIDERS stitched across its face in Old English script. The car we were staked out in belonged to a fellow gang member. I was sixteen years old.

Damien was in my gang and was down for anything. He was half-white, half-Mexican, six feet tall, with brown eyes and slicked-back dark hair. His girlfriend's jealous ex-boyfriend—the one whose house we were spying on—had just been released from jail and had, two days earlier, sworn his intention to kill Damien and me. Sitting in the borrowed car, sloshing a bottle of Olde English 800 back and forth, we were preparing to beat him to the punch.

"I still can't believe this muthafucka tried to fuck with us," Damien said. "I ain't gonna let that shit ride."

Damien was referring to the events that had taken place just two days earlier. Around 3:30 P.M. on a hot Albuquerque afternoon, Damien and I had just left his girlfriend's house and were driving down Eubank in Damien's sapphire-blue 1982 Buick Regal lowrider. Bumping Oldies music with the windows rolled down, we came to a red light. That's when a dark-gray Chevy Beretta with limousine-tinted windows pulled up inches from Damien's driver door.

"What the fuck?" Damien said.

The passenger side window rolled down. An outstretched arm holding a 9 mm handgun was now pointed at our faces.

"What's up, motherfuckers?" the ex-con, ex-boyfriend yelled.

"What the fuck you going to do, pussy?" Damien yelled back.

"I'm going to blast you and your bitch friend, motherfucker!" he said.

"Shut the fuck up, pussy!" Damien yelled.

The 9 mm pistol in his hand was the same style of weapon I'd later carry with me in Iraq, but at the moment the handgun was pointed at me. I should have kept quiet. I didn't keep quiet. Instead, I went primal.

"Do it, pussy!" I yelled. "Come on, bitch! Do it! DO IT, MOTHERFUCKER! Shoot me, you piece of fucking shit!"

Taunting an armed homicidal maniac fresh out of jail is generally a bad idea. But I wasn't smart. I was a shithead.

I yelled out my "set" (gang name).

Slowly the gun began to lower.

He knew my gang. He'd fucked up. I pressed on.

"Yeah, bitch!" I screamed through the car window. "That's right! Do it and see if you don't get blasted, you stupid motherfucker!"

The light turned green. He U-turned. We sped straight. Damien immediately dialed up his girlfriend to warn her and tell her what had just happened. More phone calls were made, guns and cars were supplied, and before we knew it, we were armed and sitting in a car in broad daylight, dressed like the hoodlums we were, just three homes from the would-be assassin's house.

Two hours. That's how long we waited—the first day, that is. The next day, we faced more of the same: no homicidal ex-boyfriend, no one to shoot and kill. Inside my sixteen-year-old shithead mind this was about honor and protection. This was something worth dying for. But whether he saw us and left or whether he had been tipped off in advance, the person we had come for never appeared. Sometimes when I lie down at night, my mind rewinds to that exact moment. There I am, sitting in that car with that gun, an insecure, violent, cocky, disgraceful little sixteen-year-old punk. I want to reach through time and kick my own ass. I want to scream at him: "What the *fuck* are you about to do? This isn't worth dying for. Turn around! There's more for you; this isn't what God put you here to do. Go home!"

But I can't do that. And even if I could, it haunts me to know it likely wouldn't have done any good.

Many years later, long after I'd left gang life and been given the privilege and honor of becoming a U.S. Marine, I learned that the ex-con boyfriend who'd sworn he'd kill us got killed in a gang shooting. That would have been my fate had it not been for the United States Marine Corps. Of this I am certain.

All I am or ever do, I owe to my beloved Corps.

I'M NOT SURE I have a good answer as to how a kid with solid and supportive parents fell into the gang life so young. But what I do know is that ever since I can remember, I have dreamed of being on the battlefield. That's true of a lot of military brats. I craved adventure, and that's one thing gang life is never short on. Growing up on Fort Bliss in El Paso, Texas, my childhood friend Abe and I played "war" with the neighborhood boys every single day after school. We were four years old and already seasoned "playground warriors." Our childhood was the type that would horrify a child psychologist, but military brats would call it normal. My friends and I lived in the worn-out cammies (camouflage uniforms) our mothers bought us from the local PX (post exchange) and scribbled pictures of tanks, jets, troops, and rifles in tropic scenes. It was great. The parents of future Olympians ship their kids off to training centers at ridiculously young ages. Earl Woods had Tiger gripping a putter straight out of the womb. So I guess you could say that base life was my military training ground.

When my neighborhood buddies and I weren't slow-creeping through brush in anticipation of ambushes, sprinting to invisible chopper LZs (landing zones), or pumping imaginary rounds from our blue toy M-16 rifles into enemy chests, we were sitting in front of a television mesmerized by my childhood idol, John Rambo. That movie influenced me so much that as a kid I tried unsuccessfully to copy Rambo's chest scars. Mom's butter knife never could get the job done.

All my earliest childhood memories are related to the military. My dad being a soldier in the Army only fueled my desire to serve. Growing up military, every day was a blur of cool military vehicles whizzing by, tough-looking men in serious-looking uniforms, aircraft rumbling overhead, and powerful weapons carried by our fathers. Generations of American boys have grown up playing with G.I. Joes, plastic green Army men, and toy guns, but the military bug had bitten me unusually young and unusually hard. I remember being five years old and asking God to please let Rambo pick me up in a helicopter so we could go on missions together in misty jungles. For the life of me I couldn't understand why the armed forces had yet to recruit me. Not having finished kindergarten seemed like such a technicality.

Being consumed by all things military was also a family affair. Even my mom got in on the action. I used to sit in my bedroom on an olive drab cot while my mother and father set up a slide projector. My mom would flick off the lights before gripping the little projector clicker. I'd sit there wearing my ragged cammies as she advanced through slide after slide of friendly and enemy aircraft (most of the latter were Chinese- and Soviet-made). The images would flash up on my bedroom wall, large and in color. When an enemy aircraft would pop up on the screen, I would pretend that I shot it down with an antiaircraft (AA) gun. As part of his job, my dad had to memorize and be able to identify aircraft instantly.

"Hind Dee."

Click.

"Mig."

Click.

"Tornado."

Click.

"F-18."

Click.

"F-16."

My mom then called out Dad's official time. Some nights these "family bonding" sessions lasted hours.

When I turned six, my father was ordered to Kirtland Air Force Base in Albuquerque, New Mexico. The house the Army put us up in was less than a quarter mile from a hangar that housed a fighter-jet squadron. This was back when the movie *Top Gun* was huge. So when I saw the movie with my new friends from across the street, Charles and Richard, we got a brilliant idea: We should sneak into the jet hangar. Dodging sentries as we went, we somehow made it all the way to the jets and actually touched the aircraft and missiles. (Thank God government facilities are better guarded now!) Our plan to get into a cockpit was cut short when an ordnance technician started yelling and chasing us. We narrowly escaped capture and later bragged to all our friends that we had flown the jets.

My earliest understanding of *actual* warfare came in 1991 with the first Gulf War. I was in fifth grade and a few guys in my class liked playing war and some even had their own green jungle boots. I bugged the hell out of my poor parents for a pair of my own, which they picked up at Kaufman's, a surplus store. Once the war broke out, and images of bruised POWs began popping up everywhere on TV, I started watching the news. Unlike *Rambo,* this was real. I tuned in daily to see what would happen to the twenty-one Americans being held hostage. I think that's when war began morphing from fantasy into reality for me. My neighborhood friends and I had spent our time watching war movies, exploring the flight line near our homes, and getting as close as we could to the hangars to steal glimpses of the gargantuan C-130s, sleek F-16s, and even the

occasional Stealth Fighter that came and went. But now I was beginning to connect the dots. The POWs on TV were somehow connected to those aircraft. The sound of F-16s taking off now began to
take on new meaning.

I lost and gained friends on a regular basis. It was just a part of
military life. The relationships and memories all stay with you, but
the whereabouts of those friends and what happens to them just
fade away. Living like a nomad forces you to learn how to hitch and
unhitch yourself emotionally from people and surroundings. When
I entered middle school, I found it all too easy to hook up with a
new crew and quickly integrate myself with the new culture.

My new best friend, Angel, was a tough kid from a bad neighborhood called "The Kirt." Angel was a dark-skinned Mexican
American kid who taught me an essential lesson in Hispanic culture: Mexicans weren't supposed to part their hair. He said his older
cousin had taught him that, and he urged me to slick my hair back
along with him. I had never had any problems with my hairstyle
and even kind of liked it, but now I couldn't believe I had been
oblivious to this important rule. So, on the last day of sixth grade,
the decision was made: We would show up on the first day of seventh grade with our hair slicked back with a fade. I spent that summer reading *Lowrider* magazine and training my hair back with a
woman's knee-high stocking that I wore while sleeping. To this day,
I still read *Lowrider* magazine. But the knee stocking hair thing was
ridiculous.

On the first day of school, I proudly met Angel and a bunch of
other Mexican kids, who all had slicked back their hair. Then I noticed my friend Jerome had changed, too. A skinny, short black kid
with short hair and a reputation for not giving a fuck about consequences, Jerome was now dressed from head to toe in red clothes and
walked with a small group of black kids from Angel's neighborhood

who also wore all red. Standing not far from us was another group of black kids, but they were wearing all blue. They had issues with Jerome and his crew.

This was my first real exposure to the Bloods and the Crips. Things went downhill immediately. Kids flashed gang signs, yelled out their "sets," and then started shoving one another. The school staff quickly broke it up, and when the bell rang, everyone was forced to disperse.

At lunch, Angel's older cousin and a group of older Mexican kids told us that if anyone messed with us during the year, they would take care of it. Angel's cousin said our newly formed group of a dozen or so Mexicans should agree to have one another's backs. And that's how fast it happened. By the end of the first day of seventh grade, I was part of a crew.

I soon took to wearing gangster gear—Nike Cortez, heavy starch creased jeans, white T-shirts, and Mad Doggs or Locs (sunglasses). I wasn't in a gang yet, but I was headed in that direction. It started off with jumping guys and starting shit with other kids. But it wasn't all just fighting. In my English class, I'd met Kevin, an upper-middle-class white kid who lived in a nice area of Albuquerque. He didn't look the part. He had hazel eyes, longer, nicely styled light brown hair and looked like he should be at a country club somewhere being an asshole to a waiter. But in reality, he was one of the most skilled "taggers" (graffiti artists) in the southeast section of Albuquerque. Kevin taught me his style. I taught him mine. And from that point on, a friendship was born.

Since we weren't eighteen yet, Kevin's older cousin would buy some of our "art supplies." It was illegal for minors to buy Magnum 44 markers. Tagging and sniffing were near epidemic. At night, we would sneak out of our houses and meet up at the Taco Bell on Gibson Street right outside the base gate and spend the whole night "bombing" the southeast section of the city. We would take turns bringing backpacks full of spray paint. We bombed school buses, apartment buildings, fences, Dumpsters . . . You name it, and we bombed it.

I started getting high, too. The first time I smoked weed, I was thirteen years old. Unfortunately, these days it's not all that uncommon for kids to start doing drugs at such a young age. But my experience was uncommon in that I was getting high with the Rollin 30s Crips.

I went over to my friend Marvin's apartment in a housing project called Mountain View Apartments. Marvin was a black kid whose skinny frame and puffy Afro made him look like a walking microphone. Hanging out at Marvin's apartment were his cousin Tyrone, who had spent time in and out of county jail; Tyrone's friend De Andre, a hulking six-foot black guy with bulging muscles and tattoos that snaked around his forearms and up his biceps; and two girls I'd never met. De Andre broke out a three-foot water bong. The thing looked like an octopus, with enough "tentacles" sticking out that everyone could toke at once. He packed the bowl with half a nickel of chronic.

"Is dat shit seeded, Cuz?" Tyrone said while punching De Andre.

"Who do you think I am, muthafucka?" De Andre said. "I already muthafuckin' did that shit last muthafuckin' night, Cuz!"

Tyrone and De Andre said "Cuz" at the end of every other sentence.

"Hit that shit as hard as you muthafuckas can, iiight, Cuz?" De Andre said.

"Iiight. But we need some music up in this bitch," Tyrone said. "Put on some Brotha Lynch Hung, Cuz!"

Music started booming. Tyrone sat down, looked at Marvin and me, and smirked.

"Li'l muthafuckas is about to get *dooooown!*"

I knew I was about to shove myself through another door lead-ing straight to a gangster's life. Mad dogging and scrapping with guys were one thing. But drugs, even just weed, were another. I knew damn well how my old-school parents felt about drugs. They preached about the evils of drugs all the time. My mom was so para-noid that I might do drugs that she'd taken to randomly accusing me of being high at the oddest times. I'd never even touched the stuff at that point, but she'd accuse me of it anyhow. I don't know. But all I remember thinking was, *If I'm going to get accused of it, I might as well get stoned* (brilliant logic, I know).

"Now you muthafuckas hit that shit!" Tyrone shouted.

We all grabbed a tentacle from the party bong and clamped our mouths down onto the tubes and sucked as hard as we could. The once-green chronic now burned a hot bright orange. Smoke raced into my lungs until it hurt. That's when I started coughing uncon-trollably. For the next twenty minutes, the room turned into a blur of faces, a pet dog, lyrics about shooting rival gang members, and the word "cuz" punctuating every other sentence the Crips spoke. The time had then come for De Andre and Tyrone to sex up the two girls.

"Iiight, li'l muthafuckas. It's time for you two to leave."

So Marvin and I left.

From then on, blazing chronic became standard. Whenever Kevin and I would plaster the city with our graffiti, we'd pack a bowl and blaze. When he and I weren't tagging, I was hanging out with Felipe, a Hispanic kid I met in seventh grade who belonged to an extremely violent street gang. After a month, his homies all de-cided that I should become a member. That's when I received an ass-beating that, up until I joined the Corps, was as rough as anything I'd ever experienced. Eight or so of us were outside drinking beer at a member's house one afternoon when they decided to rank me into the gang. I was sitting there, totally unsuspecting, when I was knocked off my chair. A blizzard of fists and Nike Cortez and Chuck Taylor sneakers hit me from every side. I fought back as hard as I could, but they were all older and stronger and they had me outnumbered. It lasted a few minutes. The only reason I know that is because a girl who was present told me so.

The weirdest part came next. After the flurry of violence, each member respectfully and sincerely shook my hand. I was now officially one of them. My problems were now their problems, and vice versa. It felt really good. If anybody fucked with me, I now had backup. I felt like I belonged.

That night, when I went home, my face looked like a balloon had inflated itself under my cheekbone. I had a slight black eye and bruises all over my body. When I got in the shower and the water hit my ribs, I thought they would crack. I got in bed and fell asleep before my parents made it home.

I spent the rest of the summer hanging out with gang members and riding around looking for trouble. The fights were brutal, ending with black eyes, broken noses, and cracked skulls. Jumping people, tagging hundreds of walls, and stealing cars—this was how I spent the summer before my eighth-grade year. I was desperate to be considered "hard" and to be "down." It was all insecurity. I was looking for a shortcut to get respect. It wasn't my gang's fault. I could have easily sidestepped the whole scene. If anyone had an "excuse" for turning out rough, it was the guys in the gang with phantom fathers. No, it was something within me—a needy desire to get the respect that is so important to males in my community. My dad was respected. My grandfather was respected. But they had *earned* it. They were *worthy* of it. They were men of honor and integrity who displayed peerless self-discipline and self-control. I didn't think

I was or ever could be like them. And even if I could, I didn't want to wait. I wanted respect now.

On the first day of eighth grade, I learned just how paper-thin friendships could be where gang life was involved. When I met up with Angel, I told him I'd joined a gang. Worse, I told him I'd joined a gang that had a beef with the gang he had joined over the summer. He instantly denounced our friendship. And just like that, we had become bitter enemies.

"Fuck you, then!" I shouted.

"No, fuck *you*!" he shot back.

You have to understand the mentality of a gangster. The gang becomes bigger than any friendship; I know cousins who have fought each other because they were from rival gangs. Since I was now an official rival of Angel's gang we could no longer be friends.

I thought we were about to get down right then and there. But we went our separate ways. Throughout the year, anytime we'd see each other there was tension. It sucked knowing how tight we'd been and that that was now finished. If I saw him in the hall, he would go out of his way to bump me hard. "I hate that fool Marco," he'd say out loud to nobody in particular. "I'm going to fuck him up."

Midway through the year is when it finally happened. Lunch period was ending and Angel and another guy I didn't like, Mark, hit me up.

"What's up, pussy?" Mark said.

"Go get a haircut, bitch!" I shouted.

Mark had scraggly hair for which he was always being teased. He promptly shut up. Angel then picked up where he left off. A small crowd of popular kids began gathering around us. I tried to remain cool. I even turned my back and started to walk back to class.

"I knew you were a pussy," Angel muttered.

"Oooooohhhhhh!" went the crowd.

I froze in midstep, turned around, dropped my books, and squared off with him. We circled once. I then snapped off a punch straight to his mouth. He held his blood-covered lip. A hard right to his stomach doubled him over. This was followed by another two strikes to his face and one back down to the stomach. Blood covered my fists and splattered the cement. Just as I went in for another blow, two teachers yanked us away from each other and rushed us off to the principal's office. A nurse said closing Angel's lip would require stitches.

Angel got three days' suspension and was picked up by his mom. I, on the other hand, had picked the single worst moment imaginable to be a shithead. When the school called my dad to come get me, he was in the middle of a general's inspection. The sergeant major answered the telephone. My dad was pulled out of formation—fucking *formation*!—to come get my dumb ass. He was livid. Not only had my behavior disappointed him, but my lack of discipline reflected poorly on our family and prevented him from fulfilling his duty.

MY GANGSTER LIFESTYLE caught the attention of the school staff. They enrolled me and all the other shining stars like me in a police-run program called G.R.E.A.T. (Gang Resistance Education And Training). They'd pull you out of class and explain the dangers of gang life. But mostly the cops were gathering intel, since they knew kids were quick to brag about their gangs.

More significant were the efforts of my Vietnam-veteran math teacher, Mr. Johnson. Mr. Johnson was the kind of guy who *looked* like he'd been to war. He had a white, ragged, tired-looking face, salt-and-pepper thinning hair, and a mustache that looked like it might have once been in style but was now, well, not. Shortly after I was ranked into my gang, Mr. Johnson began noticing a change in me. He had started and led an ROTC/CAP program. One day after class he pulled me aside, kicked the stragglers out of the room, and shut the door.

"You are going to be a part of my program whether you like it or not," Mr. Johnson said. "You best square yourself away, Mr. Martinez. Inside of you I can see a leader. What the hell are you doing with your life? You want to be a loser shitbag all your life like all those punk-ass kids you hang around with? Do you? You are joining my ROTC program and that's it! You will be a squad leader. Now pull your head out of your ass and get with the program!"

I don't know what my life would be like today without that intervention. It didn't stop me dead in my tracks or make me quit being the shithead I'd become. But looking back, I see it mattered. It jolted me. That a man who'd been to hell and back would take the time to talk some sense into me meant more than he knew. No matter how hard I ever tried to run from it, the allure of military service always seemed to stalk and track me down like a recruiter under quota.

As part of the program, Mr. Johnson had me raise the colors each morning and take them down when school let out. Across the street from the school was a retirement home where several veterans now lived. A few weeks into my new duties, I started noticing something. Some of the old men would watch me from their porch. Each day, there they were. Some would stand at the position of attention (POA). Others would salute. But each day they were there.

Once, I ran the flag up incorrectly and a couple of the old warriors hobbled across the street to correct me. "You have to understand what the flag means to them, Marco," Mr. Johnson explained to me. "It's what they fought for. Don't mess it up again."

There was no escaping Mr. Johnson's watchful eye. He knew my kind well enough to know that only through staying on top of me would I ever have a chance of being anything. He had also taken a part-time job at the PX, so he always ran into my parents and gave them a status report. America owes a great deal to our Vietnam vets, but I owe that one personally.

DESPITE MY SUSPENSION and all my gang activities, my parents remained in the dark about much of what I did. So it came as something of a shock to them when I got caught shoplifting at the PX. This was actually a mild offense compared to what I was normally up to at night, but what made the infraction bad was that I was in the store *with my father* when I decided to lift a CD. Everything was going fine and I thought I was getting away with it until a woman at the store asked me to come with her. She followed behind me to make sure I didn't dump the CD. My dad saw what was going on, but I could tell he didn't understand what was happening. He met us at the back of the store. A tough-talking MP (military police) began searching me right in front of my dad. Inside, I knew my father had to have been rooting for me to have been wrongly accused. I could tell he didn't believe his only son would stoop to stealing. *Go ahead and prove them wrong, son,* he must have been thinking. *Show them that our family has more honor than to steal.* The MP pulled the stolen CD out of my pants. I'll never forget my father's face and eyes. It wasn't a look of anger, like when he'd been pulled out of formation to pick me up for fighting. It was something far worse. It was profound disappointment. Had my father known the severity of my gang activities and how deep my delinquency went, I sometimes wonder if he would have died of a broken heart.

My theft got my father in trouble with his first sergeant. We had to go to court. It was the ultimate humiliation, as my dad had to wear his uniform. I was sentenced to counseling. My parents grounded me for the entire summer. The only day I was allowed to leave the house was the one day a week that I had to walk five miles each way to the counseling center. I and the other shitheads had to express ourselves and talk about our feelings. I hated the expressing feelings part more than the walking.

You'd think I would have straightened up. Instead, I only got worse. Before long I was back with my homies. I'd kick it with Marvin at Mountain View. We'd hang out with thugs much older than us and stroll down Central Avenue, a heavily trafficked area where everyone in the city would cruise. We'd pick out people walking and attack them. Four or five of us would bum rush the person and administer a vicious beating before snatching his money. Black eyes and split-open soft tissue were common. And for what? So we could buy forty-ounce bottles of Olde English 800?

My guilty conscience was starting to creep up on me. I decided during my ninth-grade year to get a legitimate job to earn legitimate money. This would also help out with my parents' tight finances. Raising triplet girls on an Army Ranger's salary wasn't easy. But my parents were too proud to accept handouts. My mother and father had always taught us the importance of hard work and doing every task to the fullest. I hoped getting a job would show my parents that the lesson took and that my work ethic matched theirs. I got a special license through the Labor Department that allowed a minor to work. When I got hired working at the International House of Pancakes (IHOP), my parents glowed with pride. It was a simple busboy job, but you'd have thought I told them I'd been accepted to Princeton. For the first time in a long time, they said how proud they were of me. It's amazing how something so simple meant so much—to them and to me.

But even though I was earning legit money, I still had hoodlum business ventures on the side. That was where the real money was. Me and some other kids at school had a full-scale business selling stolen car stereos and bottles of liquor. We'd walk around Albuquerque High School with clanking bottles of alcohol in our backpacks. (Later, we realized that wrapping a thin towel around the bottles minimized the clinking orchestra coming from our bags.) News spread fast. Liquor orders came in faster than we could steal product. My main business associate was Damien, whom I've already mentioned. When we told people that we'd have to suspend orders temporarily due to dwindling supply, it sparked a fierce bidding war. That was a crash course in microeconomics. Prices skyrocketed. *This sure beats the hard work at IHOP,* I thought.

Having extra funds would help with the ladies. Albuquerque girls seemed to love the whole gangster image, and I sometimes wondered whether the reason we did what we did was to attract girls. I was sixteen years old when I got my gang tattoo, an outward sign for girls and others that I belonged to a gang. A member did the tattoo for me with a prison-style tattoo machine. It reads Mi Vida Loca ("my crazy life"), a gang saying that dates back to the 1960s.

One of the downsides to gangbanging was that many of the girls I'd hook up with or date had ex-boyfriends who were either in jail, in a gang, or in a gang and in jail. And, not surprisingly, most were jealous and possessive. It wasn't uncommon to get mad-dogged by an ex-boyfriend—which included dirty looks and vulgar verbal exchanges usually followed by physical attacks or, as happened to me once, finding yourself on the wrong side of a 9 mm Beretta. Even when girls weren't at issue, you could still find yourself staring down the barrel of a gun.

Cruising down Central Avenue could be either the most enjoyable experience of a lifetime or one of the most lethal. If you liked

lowriders, Central was paradise. All years of sixties Impalas, both
hardtop and convertible, with chrome undercarriages and custom
interiors were on constant parade. The same went for all years of
Cadillacs, which were also in full force. But no matter the make or
model, almost every car on Central had two things in common: candy
paint with metal flakes and "hitting switches"—that is, switches
that activate the hydraulic suspensions and send the cars bouncing.
You couldn't turn your head without seeing a car three-wheeling,
hitting corners, hitting pancake, or jumping the front. Car clubs
were in full force. And carloads of pretty girls were everywhere.

One night I was soaking it all in, admiring the cars, when out of
nowhere I hear, "What the fuck you looking at, puto?" I'd honestly
been in a little bit of a daze. The comment startled me. I lifted my
eyes off a car I'd been admiring and looked at the twenty-something
gangster who'd yelled at me and was now throwing up hands wanting
to fight. He thought I was mad-dogging him, when, in actuality, I'd
merely been admiring cars that happened to be in his general direction. Something as simple as that, a glance that lingered too long,
was enough to spark gunplay.

He threw me some gang signs. I showed him mine. My friends
and I drove off five minutes later. A car pulled up and slung around
beside us. I thought my eyes were playing tricks on me. It was the
jealous ex-con boyfriend whose house we'd staked out in the hopes
of killing him. He'd apparently gotten wind of our plan. This wasn't
about intimidation. He was here for retaliation. The second I saw
him, I knew Damien and I were fucked.

We were driving fast. He sped up. When he and his car got par-
allel with our car, the window rolled down.

"GUN!" I yelled.

An orange burst came from the Beretta 9 mm pointing at us.

"Stay down! Get down!" I yelled.

We all got as low as we could. Even the driver was crouching as we raced down Central.

Tink. Tink. Tink.

"Fuck!" someone inside the car yelled. "Get on the freeway!"

The driver jerked the car at the last possible second onto the I-25 ramp.

In total, the whole thing lasted only a minute. But it was yet another example of stupid shit that could get you shot in the blink of an eye—and for nothing.

MY DAD RETIRED from the Army toward the end of my ninth-grade year. He was on a three-month terminal leave and wasn't actively looking for work. Somehow he thought he could support a family of six on $1,200 a month. He decided that when school let out for the summer, we would move to Texas, where he had family and land. But all I knew was that I didn't want to move to Texas. I contemplated running away. I even made plans with a friend whose mother said I could live with them on the west side of Albuquerque and attend West Mesa High School. My dad wisely maintained the element of surprise by not letting any of us know if and when we were actually moving. Either way, I figured I'd have time to say good-bye to my friends. Then one morning, without warning, my dad announced we were moving to Texas.

When we got to Olton, Texas, I saw cousins I hadn't seen in two years. I was starting to warm to the idea of a new place and a fresh start. My dad had purchased some land near Eagle Pass, Texas, and for a time thought we might move there. But that plan fell through when there was no work to be found. For the next few months, we were literally homeless. We showed up at my father's nephew's home unannounced. They lived in El Indio, population approximately thirty. The heat was unlike anything I'd ever felt—until Iraq. Worse, a stagnant canal ran through the small community and was a mosquito factory. Within hours, my parents, sisters, and I were so riddled with bites that we looked like we'd contracted chicken pox. The house had no air-conditioning and might as well have been an insect exhibit. Packs of stray dogs roamed wherever they pleased and had so many ticks covering them that they looked like they wore armor. Illegal Mexicans crossed through the town regularly and made a habit of hiding out in abandoned houses. One night, a tarantula-sized spider bit me while I slept on the floor and left pus-filled welts that oozed when I lanced them.

Soon my father announced that we were moving to his aunt's house in Del Rio. This was a vast improvement. Now we'd have fourteen people living in a two-bedroom, one-bathroom home. But after my dad still couldn't find work, my mom, who had opposed the Great Texas Adventure from the very beginning, convinced my father to move back to New Mexico. We ended up in Las Cruces. Once there, we lived with another aunt in a three-bedroom house with thirteen people. I started school shortly thereafter and we remained without a home for another two months until my father found a job as a security officer at a steel mill.

My parents begged me to stay away from the gangster life. Now that we were in a new place, they said, I had a fresh start and a clean slate. I nodded as they spoke and within two weeks was back to my old shithead ways. I made friends with a guy named Alex who became my best friend. Alex was a husky six-foot Mexican guy with light-brown skin, brown hair, and hazel eyes. He was tough. Best of all, Alex had his own apartment. He introduced me to the members of his gang, whom I befriended, and soon we were out jumping people and getting into the same old trouble I had in Albuquerque.

One of those incidents happened when another guy from their gang, Ray, and I decided to go cruising the city on a Saturday night. Ray had a lowrider Cadillac, slicked-back jet-black hair, and green eyes. Riding along, we'd ventured into a rough, poor section of town called Mesquite. A Chevy Silverado Z71 truck started following us and then drove on by. Ray stopped to talk on his cell phone when the truck circled back around and drove up to us and rolled down its window. The face staring at us was totally unfamiliar to either of us, but that didn't stop him from starting shit with Ray. This was the same kind of "swing your dick around just because you're pissed off at the world" bullshit that we'd engaged in all our lives. But now we were on the receiving end of it. Ray and the guy were shouting back and forth when suddenly the guy brandished a pistol.

"GO! GO! GO!" I yelled.

Ray slammed the gas. We got up to 60 mph in record time, but the truck was in fast pursuit. Shots rang out and Ray swerved in and out of lanes and around cars.

"We've got to lose this asshole!" he said.

More shots were fired and now Ray was randomly yanking lefts and rights down backstreets.

"HOLY FUCK!" yelled Ray.

The back windshield exploded and sent tiny glass cubes flying everywhere.

"FUCK! Lose this muthafucker, Ray!" I yelled.

The truck kept barreling after us. Ray even went the wrong way on a busy one-way street (Lohman) for a while before deciding to take the fight to his turf—Ray's gang's neighborhood, Chiva Town—English translation: "heroin town." Some friends were kicking it on the stoop of a house when we came racing up in Ray's Caddy. We were driving so fast that we came to a sliding stop. That's when our friends sitting on the stoop began firing their guns into the truck. Having people shooting at his truck apparently surprised him, because he fled the scene immediately.

When we inspected Ray's car, we found two bullet holes near the driver's door handle, five holes in the trunk area, and two in the dashboard just inches from where I had been sitting. A month or so later, members of our gang found out who had shot at us and caught up with him and his friends at Frenger Park near Las Cruces High School. When a fight erupted, Ray was there and ended up shooting two people with a shotgun. Ray, who had a young daughter, got five years in prison. After that, the group never really hung out on the regular. Alex moved to Santa Fe, New Mexico; others got thrown in jail, and still others were serving time on house arrest. The night Ray shot our attackers, I was on a date and missed the entire thing.

Even as I write about all these things, I still shake my head in disbelief. I can't understand my stubbornness or why it took me so long to realize what a mess I'd made of my life. I don't have some "moral of the story" insight into why I was the way I was or why I did the things I did. All I know is that God was bigger than my foolishness. And for whatever reason, He kept me alive for a reason. I guess what I'm saying is that, as impossible as it may seem, people can change.

Unfortunately for me, second chances weren't enough. I needed third, fourth, and fifth chances. But more than that, I needed a force capable of obliterating what I once considered "tough," "hardcore," and "badass." I needed men who ate punks like me for breakfast to kick-start my ambition and forge me into salvageable steel. I needed Staff Sergeant Marquez.

2

Going Grunt

When he walked through my high school hallway, he didn't notice me, but I noticed him. Marine Staff Sergeant Marquez was the first Marine I'd ever seen in person. It was an encounter I've never forgotten. The six-foot-tall, dark-skinned Mexican American USMC recruiter had a barrel chest, thin mustache, and bulging forearms. I remember feeling like he had a spotlight beaming down on him as he strode past me.

Marquez's stage entrance couldn't have come at a better time. My friend Ray's incarceration had hit me harder than I ever thought it would. Friends had gone to jail before, but Ray going away made me second-guess and reevaluate everything I'd done in my life. I had taken penitentiary chances over petty bullshit. Staff Sergeant Marquez's aura had sent a surge of worthlessness washing over me. Here was a guy of the same heritage who looked like he could snap me in two but who wasn't a gangster. Where I grew up that was rare. Every young guy I knew was engaged in shit he shouldn't have been. Seeing Staff Sergeant Marquez walk through that high school hallway made me feel like everything I'd ever done meant shit.

I went home that night and for the first time thought seriously about my future. *Future*—that was a word I seldom heard anyone mention. Where I grew up, kids didn't plan out or script their futures. We lived for instant pleasure. You want that chick? Spit game to her. You like that car stereo? Gank it. You're pissed off? Start some shit and rumble. What was easy and fast was where we wanted to be. But not that night. That night I asked myself big questions: Where was I going? What was I going to do? Knock some girl up? Work some minimum-wage job for the rest of my life? *You're a fucking loser, Marco,* I thought to myself.

I hopped in my car and drove around Las Cruces. I needed to think. Along the way, I drove past the Marine recruiter's office. I'd never noticed it before. I pulled into the empty parking lot and went window shopping for a future. I peered through the window and noticed a display with a ruck and combat gear. Behind that was a stand with pictures of other guys from Las Cruces who took the plunge and became United States Marines. There must have been sixty to seventy pictures on the board. Above the pictures the word *WARRIORS* was printed. I studied the guys in the pictures. None of them looked familiar, but all of them looked tired, edgy, and ready to whip the world.

I walked to the next window. Three posters hung on a wall inside. The first one had pictures of football players at the top and a charging Marine with an M-16 at the bottom. "Ever wonder why the Marines don't have a football team like the Army, Navy, or Air Force?" the poster read. "We're here to protect a country, not a quarterback."

The second poster also had an aggressive edge to it. "We Don't Promise You a Rose Garden," it said bluntly. The picture featured a pissed-off drill instructor chewing some recruit's ass.

The last poster read "If everybody could get into the Marines—

it wouldn't be the Marines." Between the phrases was a picture of a staff sergeant drill instructor at the position of attention with his sword.

I scanned the rest of the office. It was pretty sparse, but the pull-up bar inside grabbed my eye. I took a few steps back and glanced over at the Air Force office, which was right next door. Money for school was the theme there, along with "Aim High" Air Force posters. Driving back home, I decided that I'd visit the Army and Marine recruiters later in the week.

Because it was closest to my high school, I first went to see the Army recruiter. The Army recruitment office was connected to the Navy office. Walking up to the run-down strip mall, I glanced over at the Navy office window. It was full of posters of Navy SEALs.

The Army office had "Be All You Can Be" posters with promises of money for college. One poster stuck in my mind. It had a sniper and his spotter wearing ghillie suits standing in a tree in some dense jungle. "Money *does* grow on trees," it read.

I walked into the Army recruiter's office and was greeted by a black soldier who, if memory serves, was a staff sergeant. He started his speech. He talked of short enlistments, money for college, and plenty of opportunities to make rank.

"What do you think?" he asked.

"I want infantry," I said.

He started laughing.

"Are you crazy?" he asked, only half jokingly. "Why would you want to do something like that?"

I told him that I was also considering the Marines. That really got him going.

"What? Do you want to end up with nothing but a beat-up mini-truck with a Semper Fi bumper sticker at the end of your enlistment?" he scolded.

I told him I was looking to explore all my options. After five minutes, I decided that the Army was not right for me.

Next, I drove to the Marine office. When I was four years old, I'd seen a Marine Corps TV commercial with a tough-looking Marine who snapped a shimmering sword up close to his face. Since then, I'd been hooked. If I was going into the military, I wanted to be a Marine. But walking through the parking lot, I had a nervous feeling in my stomach. I'd only known soldiers and airmen all my life; Marines, I had heard, were insane. I took one last glance at the picture board of local WARRIORS and swung open the door. Staff Sergeant Marquez was sitting at his desk in Delta uniform.

"Can I help you?" he asked.

"I want infantry," I said.

Marquez slammed his hands down on his desk hard, making a loud thwack.

"You just motivated the shit out of me! What's your name?"

"Marco."

"Marco, are you ready to be cold, hungry, hot, tired, wet, and overworked?"

I smiled.

"Oh, shit! A quiet killer. I like that."

Right then, a gunnery sergeant, or gunny, walked in.

" 'Sup, Marquez?" said the gunny.

"This motivator walks in and the first thing he says is, 'I want infantry.' "

"No shit?" said the gunny. "It's about time a hard charger walked in here."

I didn't know if this was some sort of sales ploy. But if it was, it was working. I told him that I had also looked into the Army, even though I knew I had no interest in "being all that I could be."

"All service is good service," Staff Sergeant Marquez replied.

He offered me a seat and went over some paperwork. As it turned out, Marquez had been a grunt and so was able to answer all my questions about infantry. Because I was only seventeen years old, Marquez explained, I wasn't yet old enough to enlist, but he wanted me to promise to participate in poole functions (physical training). I gave him my word that I would and then got up and headed for the door.

"Where do you think you're going?" he demanded.

Confused, I turned around.

"Every time you come here, you will do a max set of pull-ups when you enter and when you leave."

I stood in front of the pull-up bar and grabbed the bar.

"Ready?" he said. "Go! One. Two. Three . . . Eleven. Twelve. Thirteen. Fourteen. Well, push that shit! Come on!"

I dropped to the ground.

"You didn't give it your all. Get up there again," he said.

Some sales pitch.

I mounted the bar again.

This time, I struggled until I made weird noises and turned red. Then my quivering arms gave out.

"That was good that time," Marquez said. "You gave it your all. That's what being a Marine is all about."

We shook hands good-bye. Staff Sergeant Marquez said he would be in touch and that I could stop by any time I wanted. I drove home and parked my car and sat thinking about what I was about to drop on my parents. For years, I only had bad news to report to them. I was hoping they'd receive this news differently. My mom was making dinner, and my dad was watching television.

"Mom. Dad. I have to tell you something," I said.

"What did you do this time?" my mom asked.

Who could blame her? She'd been conditioned.

"Mom. Dad. I'm going to join the Marine Corps Infantry!"

Mom looked horrified. Dad smiled. He got up from his seat, squared me up, and shook my hand firmly, something he'd never done before.

"Marco, this is the only thing that you have done that I fully support," he said.

MAKING A COMMITMENT at age seventeen to go grunt gave me time to extract myself slowly from the gangster lifestyle. It also allowed me to begin sharpening myself mentally and physically in preparation for boot camp. Aside from my parents, the only person who knew about my decision was my close friend Tony Morales. Tony was into physical fitness and was a clean, straight-up guy who could be trusted. We agreed to begin running together. I participated in poole functions, just as Staff Sergeant Marquez had instructed. Some recruiters hold bullshit poole functions with pussy-ass physical training (PT) so that the potential Marine won't get discouraged from joining. Not Staff Sergeant Marquez. He trashed us. On our runs, he'd yell, "It only gets worse from here!"

He had taken a special interest in me. In later conversations, I picked up signals that led me to think that he, too, might have been a hoodlum growing up. Hell, the guy even drove a lowrider. But looking back, I think the most valuable gift that he gave me was a sense that guys who came from where I came from could do this— that we could build a future and not just be written off. Staff Sergeant Marquez said he wanted me to be the platoon guide. He was harder on my PT and made me check in with him regularly. By the middle of my junior year, I'd quit smoking and was drifting away from gang activities. I took the ASVAB test, the standard exam every member of the military must take before entering the armed forces. Before I knew it, I was being processed at Military Entrance Processing (MEPS).

Staff Sergeant Marquez had warned me that my gang tattoo was going to be a problem. He'd tried to help me out by putting in a good word for me, but he was honest in saying that the burden of convincing the gunny that I had genuinely dropped the gangster routine would be on me.

The challenge came almost as soon as I got to MEPS in El Paso. Right after roll call was taken, I looked around the waiting room and noticed that I was the only Marine there. Everyone else was Army, Air Force, or Navy. Just when I was beginning to think my exclusivity was some sort of badge of honor, a pissed-off-looking gunny barged into the room:

"MARTINEZ!"

I jumped up and stood outside the door.

"Well, come in!" he barked.

When I walked in, he was seated behind his desk. The gunny wasn't physically large, but from the ribbons on his chest, I could tell he'd been in the Gulf War. He had a horseshoe flattop and a body like a fist, compact and hard. I stood in front of him at parade rest, just as Staff Sergeant Marquez had instructed me to do. He was a gatekeeper, a human shithead detector whose job was to weed out nonhackers and unrepentant thugs. I didn't know what I was supposed to do next, so I just shut my mouth.

"Are you some punk-ass gangster, Martinez?"

"No, Gunny."

"So then why do you have a gang tattoo?"

"I was a gangster, Gunny, but not anymore."

"Oh, so you *were* a gangster?"

"Yes, Gunny."

"Let me see this tattoo."

I pulled up my shirt and turned around. I stood there for a few seconds with my back turned to him.

"'Mi—Vida—Loca,'" he read slowly. "What does that mean?"

"It means 'My Crazy Life.'"

"Turn around."

I looked down on his desk and saw a police gang tattoo identification book. The pages had been opened to the Hispanic gang tattoos section. *Shit!,* I thought.

"Right here it says that if you have this tattoo, you're a hardcore gang member. Why should I let you in?"

"Ever since I was a little kid I wanted to be a Marine. I steered off the right path and now I want to get back on the right path. If I can't get into the Marines, I don't know what I'll do. There is nothing for me. I want to see combat. I want to come back and show people I'm not a loser."

He leaned back in his chair and gave a deep sigh. He then sat there in silence for about thirty seconds. He was both judge and jury. I awaited his verdict.

"Okay. I'll let you in. But you better not fuck up in the Marines."

"I won't, Gunny. I promise."

"Now get out of my office."

I was ecstatic, but I knew that there would be more hurdles left to clear before I was officially in the Corps. I walked back into the room with the rest of the group.

"What happened?" one of them asked me.

"It's a Marine thing," I said.

Soon the doctors called me in and began testing everything: They drew blood, made me walk like a duck, had me flail and rotate my arms, and checked my vision and hearing. When it came time for the hearing test, I sat in the booth, put on the headphones, and the test began. All I could hear was static over some beeps. When the test was over, the doctor asked if I'd ever had surgery on my ears. "No. Why?" I asked. "Because you failed the hearing test," the doctor said. "I'm afraid that disqualifies you from consideration. I'm sorry."

What the fuck am I going to do now? I thought. I hadn't even taken the ACT or SAT for college. Even if I had, it's doubtful I would have done well enough to get into a college. All that time spent acting like a fuckup had meant I didn't take school seriously. And even if I did somehow pull off a respectable score, I knew my parents didn't have the money.

I felt like shit and was just about to walk out and go home. But on a whim, I walked back over to the doctor and asked whether there was supposed to be static on the headphones. No, he said. Learning what had happened, he handed me another headset. I had another shot. This time, I passed the hearing test almost perfectly.

At the end of the day, those who passed the physical were taken into a room and sworn in by an Army captain. The room had a beautiful American flag on a brass and wood pole centered against a wall with the Marine Corps, Navy, Army, Air Force, and Coast Guard flags flanking both sides of the American flag.

"Raise your right hand and repeat after me," said the captain.

"I, Marco Martinez, do solemnly swear that I will support and defend the Constitution of the United States against all enemies foreign and domestic, that I will bear true faith and allegiance to the same, and that I will obey the orders of the president of the United States and the orders of the officers appointed over me, according to the rules and regulations and the Uniform Code of Military Justice so help me God."

It might sound stupid, but while my right hand was in the air, I felt proud. I was proud of myself, proud of my family's service, and, yes, proud of being an American. My father had pledged to defend

America before he was even officially a citizen. Maybe some people raise their right hands and swear allegiance to live and die for the Constitution lightly, as a formality or hoop they must jump through. But I don't think so. I think most people feel something when they take that oath. I know I did. And I'm not ashamed to admit it. I was finally doing something that was worth something. If I was going to get shot and killed, better for it to happen defending the country that had given my family everything rather than squabbling over girls or misinterpreting glances.

After we finished things, Staff Sergeant Marquez picked me up. He asked how things went and I told him I thought it went well. "Good. In September, we'll sign the papers," he said. "Cool," I replied.

On the drive home, Marquez told me tales of all the places he had been and the things he had done in the fleet Marine force. The fact that he had been a grunt made all the difference in the world. He knew what I'd be going through and, just as important, what drove guys like me to want to be infantrymen. When we got to my house, he said he had something for me. He handed me a package wrapped in a white T-shirt.

"You've sharpened your body," he said. "Now sharpen your mind."

As he drove off, I unrolled the T-shirt. The phrase PAIN IS WEAKNESS LEAVING THE BODY was printed on it in black letters. The package that had been wrapped in the T-shirt had a picture of three Marines, two males and one female, in dress blues. WELCOME ABOARD was printed on the front. Inside were stuffed booklets and study guides covering everything from rank structure to general orders. It became my "bible." I studied it every night.

Senior year passed quickly. Soon, I would be starting a new life with a prestigious organization with an illustrious history that had decided to take a chance on a shithead. I went to the recruiting office on my eighteenth birthday and signed the mountain of paperwork. The Marine mentality had already begun to sink in. When senior skip day came, I attended classes. When class let out, I went to the recruitment office to hang out with Staff Sergeant Marquez so he could drill me on all the materials he'd given me to study. When homecoming rolled around, instead of spending the night partying, I spent it running a physical fitness test (PFT) with Tony. Then came prom. I didn't bother to go, passing up a date. Instead, I spent the night running six miles and studying Marine knowledge.

The metamorphosis surprised even me. I'd never been passionate about anything, and rigorous studying was something I knew nothing about. But that changed. My desire to be a gangster had all but evaporated. And here's the thing: I started to see my peers in a different light. People say that service members and civilians live in worlds apart—that we necessarily see the world through different eyes. As a kid, I loved playing war and dreaming of Rambo-style adventures. But those were immature visions of combat and service. My entry into gang life had been even more unthinking, a hollow attempt to win friends, gain respect, find adventure, and feel a sense of brotherhood.

Being a Marine and being a gangster are not comparable—not even close. Anyone who tries to blur the line between the two just because they both are prepared to use violence to achieve their goals doesn't know what the fuck he's talking about. That's like saying a fireman and an arsonist are one and the same simply because they both deal in fire. That's ridiculous. Training oneself to use lethal force to save lives is not the same thing as using lethal force to destroy lives. They are exact opposites. I'll always regret being a shithead. I'll never regret being given the privilege of becoming a Marine.

HIGH SCHOOL GRADUATION night was just as much a victory for my parents as for me. I'd made it through in one piece, and somehow they'd kept their sanity. Everybody in my family was excited. I, on the other hand, was only partially excited. It wasn't nearly as special as people made it to be. During the graduation ceremony, I sat and listened to the valedictorian talk about the new adventures that awaited her and others at college. I chuckled inside, knowing that if anyone would be on an "adventure," it would be me and the others headed into the military. I looked out over the sea of robes and tassel-topped caps. People and choices now all seemed different to me. Not better or worse—just different. I had already sworn and pledged my allegiance to defend the nation from its enemies, both foreign and domestic. The only thing "foreign and domestic" on the minds of most graduates was which type of beer to drink. It felt strange.

We walked across the stage and got our diplomas. Everyone threw their caps in the air except me. I just watched, as people cried and hugged and yelled, "We did it!" I met up with my parents, who took pictures and congratulated me. I was happy that they were happy. It was their parental "finish line." And if anyone deserved to be congratulated, it was them, not me. My mom and dad said that they understood that I probably wanted to go have fun with my friends, so they left with some friends to go have dinner.

I walked through the parking lot toward home. Once on the street, I walked past parties where I saw some friends. But I didn't stop. People in cars drove by and popped champagne bottles. I kept walking. When I got home, my parents wondered why I had returned so early. I told them that I didn't feel much like partying. I closed my bedroom door and studied Marine rank structure.

A few weeks later, the big day finally arrived. I was leaving for boot camp. My family and I spent the day together. It would be the last time I would live with my parents or see them on a regular basis. We loaded up for the drive to El Paso, where I'd stay in a hotel with other Marine recruits. We said our good-byes and I told them I would see them in three months.

The next morning, activities began at 4:00 A.M. After being sworn in again, we boarded a flight to San Diego. Once there, we were instructed to find the USO in the airport. We spotted an old man wearing a Marine hat who happened to be an airport worker.

"Recruits?" he said.

"Yes, sir," we replied.

He pointed and said, "Salvation from a civilian existence is through those doors, boys."

We thanked him and headed for the doors. I was the last one through. I stopped to look back at the proud old Marine, now lost in thought and smiling at the floor.

3

House of Pain

e fell silent.

Our bus pulled up to the military police gate at Marine Corps Recruit Depot (MCRD) San Diego. It was around 8 P.M. We rumbled past the squad bays and into a paved parking lot riddled with yellow footprints. Fifteen drill instructors stood cocked and ready. The second our bus came to a halt, a DI tore up the stairs and unleashed a forty-eight-hour whirlwind known as recruit processing.

"You punk-ass motherfuckers have ten seconds to get the fuck off my bus!" he yelled.

We just looked at him blankly.

"RIGHT FUCKING NOW!"

So frantic was our movement that you'd have thought the bus had been driven into the ocean and was filling with water. We became a ridiculous tangle of limbs, personal effects, and motion. We exited the bus door and a swarm of DIs descended on us. When my first foot hit the pavement, a DI slammed his Smokey Bear brim into my face. He then grabbed me by the shirt and yelled for me to get on a pair of yellow footprints. That's when I realized it had been a mistake to arrive at boot camp with my head already shaved.

"You think you're some kind of badass, you fucking maggot?" one of the four DIs who'd now ganged up on me yelled. "You're NOTHING! You fucking worthless maggot!" another one screamed two inches from my face.

We were then told to get down on our right knee. They pointed to a sign that had the basic articles of the Uniform Code of Military Justice (UCMJ). We stayed in our knight kneel and were sworn in again. The yelling and ruffling quickly resumed. The doors on the building next to us burst open with a bang. We were hustled into the building, where all our possessions—deodorant, watches, tooth-brushes, you name it—were thrown in the trash. Bodies were patted down and heads were shaved, and before I knew it, I was standing naked in formation getting issued underwear, cammies, and shoes (boots were a privilege we'd yet to earn). From there it was off to an auditorium where we filled out endless amounts of paperwork and then sat for hours in a statue pose looking straight forward. Sleepy, bobbing heads were met with swift DI intervention.

DIs divided us into groups that would become our platoons. We were then rushed to a windowless squad bay where we made racks (beds) and marked all our gear before being ordered to clean the squad bay. As we'd soon learn, our job as recruits was to clean things—everything. We were Martha Stewarts with shaved heads, Marine maids whose job it was to maintain cleanliness and order in every conceivable nook and crevice of our squad bay. Cleaning was our mandated addiction.

Just when we started to think sleep might be near, we were com-manded to stand at the position of attention for hours. There were no windows, and none of us knew for sure what time it was. Ex-haustion and hunger were beginning to morph into blurry-eyed submission. We stood at the POA for hours before finally eating chow, which was breakfast, an apparent clue that it might now be morning. I'd pulled all-nighters gangbanging, but this was different. We were disoriented. After chow, it was back to the squad bay, where—you guessed it—we were treated to more cleaning and the chance to make a phone call to our parents. Here's how every single call went:

Ring.

"Hello? Mom? It's me. I'm in boot camp."

Then the DI slammed down the phone.

Six seconds. No more. Back to cleaning.

Then came one of the most important and telling moments of entry into the Corps. If there is one experience I wish every American could encounter, it would be this one: "The Moment of Truth." We were corralled into a small auditorium where we were instructed to, again, sit like statues. DIs circulated and kept us awake by yelling and occasionally slapping the backs of heads with a hard smack. That's when the doors exploded open and a gunnery sergeant burst through. He had a voice box like a megaphone and yelled like I had never heard anybody yell before.

"Listen up! Who wants out of this nightmare? Huh? Who here thought they could lie to the Corps? If you did, we know about it! If you lied about medical problems, lied about your past, if you lied about *anything,* we motherfucking know about it, you punk-ass motherfucking maggots! Who the fuck lied? Who the fuck wants out? It only gets worse from here. This is your only way out. If you want out, you'll be back home tonight. Tell me right fucking now! If you want out, stand up right fucking now!"

Recruits started popping up from their seats. They were taken to offices on the side of the auditorium. A mass confession that would have impressed even the Pope quickly ensued. Revelations about medical problems were a common favorite. Some may have been legitimate, but most were bogus—bullshit excuses to not have to go through with it. All the nonhackers were taken through some doors, never to be seen again. Our numbers had been significantly depleted. We hadn't even gone to sleep and already one-quarter of the recruits had quit.

But lots of others had to go into side offices also—including me. Even someone with a slight medical problem had to be questioned and examined, and the same went for anybody who had a tattoo. That damn gang tattoo. My interrogation would be conducted by a staff sergeant. These men knew gang tattoos like sports fans know jersey numbers. And unlike the gunny back at the MEPS, this man didn't need a reference manual. As soon as I rotated my torso to display my past, the staff sergeant instantly recognized my gang's markings.

"Are you a punk-ass gangster?" the staff sergeant demanded.

"No, sir."

"Then why the *fuck* do you have a gang tattoo, ass?"

"I was stupid, sir. I'm here to change my life, sir."

"Martinez, you better not fuck up my Corps."

"Aye, sir."

I'd eked through again, but the same could not be said for the guy right after me.

"What the fuck is that?" I heard the staff sergeant yell. "Is that a fucking swastika? Get the fuck out of my office, you piece of shit!" A DI quickly came and escorted anti-Semite swastika boy through the doors where all the other nonhackers went.

It was at about this point that I thought I would pass out from sleep deprivation. The DIs bet otherwise. We were shuttled off for chow, which was dinner. The DIs told us that we had an initial strength test (IST) in the morning to see if we could make it to the next phase. Luckily, I didn't have to do fire watch (guard duty) that night, so I could go to sleep. But it seemed like I had just closed my eyes when I was awoken by the clanging sound of a DI banging a trash can before body-slamming the metal cylinder to the floor.

"Move, you fucking maggots! You're not moving fast enough!" he screamed. "Get the fuck up, you fucking maggots!"

During the IST, the "all you can eat" breakfast eaters blew chunks as we ran. Others fell out completely. After the IST, all who had passed were told we would tour a real boot camp squad bay. We were seated and the receiving DI disappeared. A few minutes later, the door directly in front of us slammed open so hard it made a hole in the wall. Three DIs stood before us, two green belts and one senior, the black belt. Senior DI Staff Sergeant Yates introduced himself as our new leader. He explained that he was the definitive authority figure in our pathetic little lives and that we were the scum of the earth. He then introduced Sergeant Park and Sergeant Cunningham, both standing at parade rest in inspection perfect Charlie's. And with that, the gates of hell opened up on all seventy of us.

DI Yates left and the green belts, DI Cunningham and DI Park, yelled for us to get on line. "On line" was a literal statement. The boot camp squad bay was lined with racks on both sides of the squad bay. The racks were in a perfect line, and a long piece of tape ran the length of both sides of the squad bay. These were the lines. We hurried to jump on them. Some recruits were pushed, and others were hit for getting too close to the DIs. I was "Supermanned" into my rack—tackled for getting in Drill Instructor Sergeant Cunningham's way. Those deemed too slow were thrashed on the quarterdeck. As the night wore on, many recruits, including me, visited the quarterdeck. When I got there, the puddle of sweat looked like a bottle of spilt water. I was "trashed" until my uniform was soaked. "Trashed" is the term Marines use to describe physical exercise done to the point of profuse sweating and near muscle failure. This was our first night of actual boot camp.

That night we were schooled in the art of speaking in the third person. No longer would we say "I," "my," or anything in the first person. "I" became "this," as in "This recruit wishes to speak." Speaking in the first person was a privilege, a statement of human worth and purpose that was reserved only for Marines. We weren't Marines. We were not even humans. We were "recruits," the lowliest scum on earth. The privilege of time vanished when we got to MCRD San Diego. The only watches worn belonged to the DIs. For the next three months, our platoon lived from meal to meal, knowing only vaguely what time it was—or why we chose to make this house of pain our new home.

OVER THE FOLLOWING ninety days, DI Sergeant Cunningham would reprogram us in almost every aspect of human existence, including how to eat, speak, dress, walk, run, and sleep. Cunningham was, without question, the meanest man I've ever met. He was also one of the best drill instructors a grunt could have asked for.

The second day of boot camp started after yet another blink's-length night of sleep. DI Cunningham promised to make the squad bay rain and make the walls sweat before the day was over. He kept his word, but not before first feeding us a well-balanced, nutritious breakfast. It's rumored that you get three meals a day in boot camp. And, in a sense, that's true. It all depends on what your definition of "meal" is. Cunningham told us that we didn't rate forks or knives and that spoons would be our only utensils until we went home. When we got our food, we were instructed to scoop a spoonful and hold it in front of our faces.

"Take a bite!" DI Cunningham yelled.

We bit.

"Chew!"

We chewed.

"Swallow!"

We swallowed.

"You're done. Get the fuck out of my chow hall!" he yelled.

One bite; we were done. We got the fuck out of his chow hall.

Many meals went this way. Sometimes we were allowed to eat for ten minutes, a luxury to be sure. But you could never be sure. So you ate at warp speed and didn't talk, something we weren't allowed to do anyhow. Some civilians might think this all sounds like mindless bullshit or extreme privation. But it wasn't. As much as we all hated it, those of us who would later taste combat came to realize its value. Eating in combat was nearly impossible. Growling stomachs were something a grunt needed to learn to ignore while still performing at optimal speed.

But eating lessons weren't all we learned; the importance of controlling bowel movements was also taught in memorable fashion. Proper hydration was drilled into us. We drank bottomless canteens of water. But the DIs would not let any recruits go to the bathroom. We were on the verge of throwing up. And God help you if you did throw up, because then you had to drink the same amount of water that you'd drunk during the pre-puke session. The second week of boot camp was the only time in my life that I ever saw a grown man piss and shit himself.

A recruit had asked if he could make a sit-down head call (take a shit). "Sir, this recruit requests permission to speak to Drill Instructor Sergeant Cunningham, sir!"

"What?" said DI Cunningham.

"This recruit requests to make a sit-down head call, sir!"

"No."

"Aye, aye, sir!"

DI Cunningham started trashing the recruit. You were not allowed to ask to go to the head (bathroom) during cleanup. But that didn't stop the recruit. He asked three more times, and each time his request was denied. I was outside cleaning the cracks in the sidewalk when I heard the recruit yell, "Sir, this recruit is going to shit himself, sir!"

"Shut the fuck up!" DI Cunningham yelled back.

Minutes later, the recruit shat himself and got up from the quarterdeck and ran toward the head. DI Cunningham went berserk. The recruit started running from DI Cunningham, becoming unhinged. I looked up from the concrete cracks and saw the recruit smash his head through the window. The bloody head then disappeared as he got pulled back through the window. Word had it that well before this point the recruit was struggling emotionally and with adapting to Corps life. We never saw him again.

Being stripped of all humanity and learning to get accustomed to being treated like vermin also extended to medical care. I had always heard that all Marines love Navy corpsmen. That was true in combat, but not in boot camp. The corpsmen we dealt with treated us like shit. They went out of their way to dog us and gouge needles into us at the most painful angles possible.

But behind each hardship—one-bite meals, extreme physical exertion, controlling bodily functions, yanking the safety net of comfortable medical care out from under us—was a purpose. Trashing was never random; everything had a lesson attached to it, even if that lesson only became clear later. This was especially true for me and my fellow grunts, like Anthony Reyna, Freddy Santiago, Sean Ray, and many others who became good friends. The dividing line between POGs (pronounced "pogues"), which are non-infantry Marines, and ground pounders ("grunts," or 03s) was stark and important. DIs Cunningham and Park took a special interest in making sure we trigger pullers lived inside a hell of maximum intensity. If and when the time ever came, the 03s would need to be hard in a way POGs wouldn't. The DIs knew this, and they trained and trashed us accordingly.

"If you're an 03, get on my quarterdeck right now!" the DIs would yell. And that would ignite the trashing of a lifetime, while the POGs stood at the POA and watched. It's weird how the human body and mind learn to adapt to such things. What we worried about most was screwing up, because then a "hurricane" might find its way into our squad bay. When this happened, the DIs would tear apart the racks, rummage the whiskey lockers, close all the windows, and trash everybody until it got humid, at which time they'd turn on all the hot water in the head. Next, we'd be instructed to put on ponchos before being trashed again. And then the *real* fun would begin.

"Get on line and open your lockers! Throw everything in the middle!" a DI would yell.

We'd get yelled at for what fuckups we were and be given twenty minutes to clean up a two-hour mess. With all our personal effects now in the middle of the floor, we would scurry to get our things. If you couldn't find them, you'd have to get them later—in the middle of the night at the "recruit swap meet." After one PT session had gone bad, we were told to throw every piece of PT gear in a huge, steamy, sweat-drenched pile of T-shirts, socks, shorts, and shoes. Wearing only underwear, we were given exactly one minute to dress. It was impossible to find any of your clothes, so you'd end up pulling on someone else's sopping socks or putting your legs through some other recruit's PT shorts. Over the next few days, your new mystery clothes would begin to sour, since changing clothes and showering were not permitted.

Looking back, I see that these exercises were child's play. More than that, they served a purpose. During the invasion of Iraq, our platoon went more than a month before taking a shower. Wearing the sweat of your Marine brother was the least of your worries. It was his blood you didn't want to see spilled.

Another favorite "game" was the footlocker shuffle. If we screwed up right before bed, we'd get on line, open our footlockers, wagon wheel around at the DI's command, and then stop and hook our unlatched lock onto another footlocker. We'd do this over and over until you had no idea where your lock was. We'd then do the same with the two trays inside. By the end of the deal, you had no idea where anything was. You'd get on line, lock the lock on your footlocker, and have from 1:00 A.M. to 5:00 A.M. to have all your things back in your footlocker and locked with your original lock. What might seem like useless agitation was actually a lesson in communication; it was about restoring order in the midst of confusion. And as with everything the DIs had us do, we were acquiring skills and truths, even if we didn't always realize it at the time.

Much of our formal Marine knowledge came through the "little green monster," a book that covered every aspect of surviving boot camp. Well, not *every* aspect. I learned there were other, equally important rules to live by that couldn't be found in any book. Once, while drilling on the grinder (parade deck), DI Cunningham, who was sick as a dog, as were all of the recruits, sucked up a wad of throat mucus and gathered it in his mouth. But instead of spitting on the ground, he hocked the wad into the palm of his hand.

"Never, never spit on any parade deck," he told us. "Men that have gone to war and died have marched on the very same deck. Marines who have received the Medal of Honor have marched on this deck."

That's when I started to realize how special the organization I had joined was. DI Cunningham's passion was drill. And he approached it with lethal seriousness. But the idea that we were marching on the same parade deck as the warriors who'd come and gone before us started to sink in. It reminded me of the lineage and legacy of the Corps and what a privilege it was to suffer in the same house of pain that others before us had. Whenever we saw a white Chevy Silverado out in the parking lot, our hearts sank, because that meant DI Cunningham was onsite. But for all DI Cunningham's cruelty and harshness, he not only trained us well, he taught us to be worthy heirs of our Marine heritage.

And he had another redeeming quality: DI Cunningham had one of the most beautiful cadences (measured movement in marching) I've ever heard. He called it with a precision that matched his ruthlessness. His voice boomed, and when he called cadence, you wanted to march your very best to it—and not simply because there would be hell to pay if you didn't.

When the time came for our platoon to learn the "Marines' Hymn," I already knew it by heart, since I'd studied so much before boot camp. We'd often sing it following a hygiene inspection.

"Turn on the radio!" Cunningham would bark.

"Turn on the radio! Aye, sir!" we'd yell back.

And then, together, we would sing.

> *From the halls of Montezuma to the shores of Tripoli,*
> *We fight our country's battles in the air, on land and sea.*
> *First to fight for right and freedom,*
> *And to keep our honor clean,*
> *We are proud to claim the title of United States Marines.*
> *Our flag's unfurl'd to every breeze. From dawn to the setting sun;*

*We have fought in every clime and place where we could
take a gun.*
*In the snow of far-off northern lands and in the sunny
tropic scenes,*
*You will always find us on the job The United States
Marines.*
*Here's health to you and to our Corps which we are proud
to serve;*
In many strife we've fought for life and never lost our nerve.
If the Army and the Navy ever look on heaven's scenes,
*They will find the streets are guarded by United States
Marines.*

The "Hymn" made you feel proud and motivated. When you were tired, the "Hymn" rekindled your fire.

But my favorite motivator was the Rifleman's Creed. We'd say it on the parade deck, in the squad bay, or anywhere we held a rifle—and we held a rifle almost 90 percent of the day. The Rifleman's Creed can't be found in any recruiting brochures. And to a civilian, an ode declaring one's weapon as human and a best friend might sound crazy. But to Marines it makes perfect sense. It was the kind of thing that could make the most jaded guy motivated. DI Cunningham would yell the command:

"Rifleman's Creed!"

"Rifleman's Creed. Aye, sir!" we would boom in unison.

And then we'd begin:

*This is my rifle. There are many like it, but this one is
mine.*
*My rifle is my best friend. It is my life. I must master it as
I must master my life.*

Without me, my rifle is useless. Without my rifle, I am useless. I must fire my rifle true. I must shoot straighter than my enemy who is trying to kill me. I must shoot him before he shoots me. I will.

My rifle and I know that what counts in this war is not the rounds we fire, the noise of our burst, or the smoke we make. We know that it is the hits that count. We will hit.

My rifle is human, even as I am human, because it is my life. Thus, I will learn it as a brother. I will learn its weaknesses, its strength, its parts, its accessories, its sights and its barrel. I will ever guard it against the ravages of weather and damage as I will ever guard my legs, my arms, my eyes and my heart against damage. I will keep my rifle clean and ready. We will become part of each other. We will.

Before God, I swear this creed. My rifle and I are the defenders of my country. We are the masters of our enemy. We are the saviors of my life.

So be it, until victory is America's and there is no enemy, but peace!

While reciting the Creed, I would grip my rifle proud and tight, yelling the words at the top of my lungs. I would picture myself blowing away any enemy in front of me. I once yelled the Creed so loud that DI Cunningham had everybody stop and listen. I was in the zone, unaware that I was now the only one reciting it. DI Cunningham just nodded his head in approval as I gripped the rifle so tight that my knuckles turned white. The Creed got me so fired up that it put me in a blood lust. I wanted to kill America's enemies. I could see and taste it. The Rifleman's Creed became my motivational fuel—the thing that kept me burning throughout my four years in the Marine Corps.

FOR ALL THE unifying things we did, seventy guys living together in a squad bay was bound to create rivalries and the desire to fight. So, to avoid getting in trouble with our DIs, we set up secret gladiator fights at least twice a week, usually taking place in the rain room. You could fight anybody you wanted in the platoon. I fought once with a squad leader who had talked smack and pissed me off. "What the fuck you going to do about it?" he said. I said nothing but instead pointed to the rain room, where I proceeded to beat his ass soundly. Watching fights was like our own private boxing arena. It was also a good way to let out anger and, ironically enough, build respect and brotherhood with one another.

When we entered the second phase of training, we moved to Edson Range, located at Camp Pendleton, California. Things took a turn for the worse. Meals got smaller. Work got harder. And, for a time, we found ourselves using newspaper as toilet paper. After lunch one day, I overheard DI Cunningham talking to DI Park. "Today is the twelfth of September," he said, "so next we will start field week and we'll . . ."

I stopped listening.

Motherfucker! I said to myself. We'd been so alienated from the outside world that my nineteenth birthday had passed and I didn't even know it.

When field week came around, DI Cunningham and DI Park went out of their way to tighten the vise around grunts' nuts. On difficult assault courses, we'd have to traverse most of the way by low-crawling under barbed wire while dragging a thirty-pound ammo can until our elbows and knees bled.

"Listen up 03s!" DI Park yelled at us. "This is your life!"

Fuck, I thought to myself. *Going grunt is no joke.*

The rest of the week consisted of getting fucked with and running through an array of assault courses in preparation for the Crucible. The Crucible is unfamiliar to older Marines because it didn't come on line until the 1990s. It's the epic two-day field test that stands between a recruit becoming a full-fledged Marine. Field week was an integral part of preparing for the Crucible. And one experience that no recruit ever forgets is going through the gas chamber.

We'd already survived swim qualifications, leapt off of soaring platforms and into water, and rappelled down towers. But the gas chamber had everybody worried. When it came time for us to be gassed, we hiked up to a small brick shack. The DIs briefed us. We were to wear our gas masks into the chamber, remove them, and "don and clear" the masks before walking out. But when the DIs put on the full protective gear known as MOPP suits (Mission Oriented Protective Posture), we knew we were about to chomp down on a shit sandwich. The DIs entered the chamber and ignited tablet after tablet of CS gas. Smoke poured out from every opening in the shack. I was in the middle of the line. Five minutes later, gasping, coughing, hacking creatures emerged from the brick building with tear- and snot-covered faces.

When it was finally my group's turn, we donned and cleared our gas masks. The room was so full of smoke I could hardly see. We were instructed to take our masks off then put our backs against the wall. My hands started to itch. My eyes felt like they'd been soaked in Mace. Ten seconds went by. Then twenty. Then forty. I was almost out of breath when finally I heard someone start coughing, setting off a chain reaction. I breathed the rancid air. The thick gas burned in my lungs. I doubled over, coughing uncontrollably.

"Control it, Martinez! Control it!" SDI Yates yelled.

I tried, but it was pointless. I squinted at the exit. If you ran, you had to do it all over again. I was now in a bit of a panic. I guess Yates thought I was going to make a run for it, so he slammed me into the wall, causing me to stand straight.

"Don and clear!" he yelled.

When we donned and cleared, we were all still coughing inside our masks. But we finally began to gain composure. We had survived being gassed.

Or so we thought.

"Okay, we're going to do it one more time," SDI Yates announced. "Unmask!"

We did the whole thing again. When we were finished, our faces looked like we'd walked through spiderwebs made of snot. As I was wiping my face clean I indulged in the luxury of clean air. *This would make one helluva recruiting poster,* I thought—a picture of a mucus-glazed recruit with a tagline that reads, THE MARINES: WE'LL MAKE YOU APPRECIATE CLEAN AIR.

Leading up to the Crucible, we also went through primary marksmanship instruction (PMI). When it came time to qualify on the rifle, I was one of about eight who qualified expert. It was always funny to see who could shoot and who couldn't.

The night before the Crucible, DI Cunningham had us iron on the coveted Eagle, Globe, and Anchor on our cammies. Most of us were eager and ready for the Crucible. The sleepless two and a half days sucked. But by that point, most of us were so hungry to become Marines that we didn't care. We hiked over twenty-five miles, completing stations and assault courses along the way. The morning of the Reaper Hike, I fell asleep while hiking. I was sleephiking. Many people fell out of the hike, and still more fell out when we started up the Reaper's sharp incline.

But when we got to the top, it felt good—damn good. The

Eagle, Globe, and Anchor were handed out to each recruit. Some pussies cried. Cobra helicopters flew overhead during the ceremony, as a group of old Marines sat atop the Reaper and watched it all unfold.

The strangest part of the Crucible for a grunt is that what at the time seems like the most grueling experience ever soon morphs into an easy, shoulder-shrug experience. The shit we had to do post-Crucible was far worse. Today I look back on my Crucible and smile; we were so damn naïve. We thought that was hell personified. We had no idea.

We returned to MCRD San Diego and prepared for our ten-day leave. When I stuck my ATM card into the machine to check my balance, I was disappointed to see I had less than $750 for three months' work.

Boot camp graduation day was special, but our DIs made sure to remind us that our Eagle, Globe, and Anchor didn't mean we weren't still maggots. The night before the ceremony, they made us drink water until we puked. The morning of our graduation ceremony, they trashed us no different than if it had been our first day of boot camp. We then got into our Deltas and formed outside with the rest of the company as the crowd of spectators swelled.

Five minutes before we were to graduate, DI Cunningham, the meanest DI of the three, shared tender words of inspiration and good cheer, as he sent us off to whip the world: "Not one of you better talk to me after this shit's over! I fucking hate all you weak-ass motherfuckers! I don't want to ever see you maggots ever again! I will always be 'sir' to you!"

The signal sounded and we marched.

4

FUBAR

Boot camp leave ended quickly, and before I knew it, I found myself doing the "sea bag drag" through the El Paso airport and then over to San Diego Airport before shuttling to Camp Pendleton. We had to report in Alphas, but I noticed that many Marines looked like a bag of ass. Their uniforms were all screwed up with improper placements of simple things that are hard to mess up. DI Cunningham had taught us well. When we showed up at the School of Infantry (SOI), those of us who had trained under him were complimented on having outstanding uniforms.

SOI was both a reunion with my grunt boot camp buddies and also a new phase of Marine life. Becoming an infantryman would demand endless hikes and deepening one's love affair with his rifle. When the salt-and-pepper-haired SOI sergeant major gathered all the incoming students for a first-day discussion, he made it crystal clear that nonhackers would not be tolerated. We sat in bleachers and listened.

"Gents," he said, "this is the real deal. This is SOI. You are no longer guaranteed a certain amount of sleep. See those hills?"

He pointed to Camp Pendleton's mountainous terrain.

"You will be hiking those hills for miles with a full combat load. This is going to challenge you more than boot camp ever could. Who here thinks they can't make it?"

A new Marine stood up.

"Sir, I don't think that I can make it, sir!"

"Why not, Marine?" the sergeant major asked.

"My shoulders hurt when I carry a pack, Sergeant Major."

"Get out of the bleachers and go to the administration building. We don't need nonhackers."

The embarrassed Marine quickly made his way off the bleachers and left.

"Anybody else?"

Silence.

"Good training starts in two days. Dismissed!"

"Good training." That's a phrase Marines know well. It refers to anything that does not kill you. Before good training began, we were put into three platoons. I was in Alpha company, 1st Platoon. During boot camp, your focus is on survival. Building strong bonds with your brothers happens largely in silence, because every word, movement, and spoonful of food is controlled and scripted by your DIs. SOI was physically hardcore, but it also gave you the chance to look up and around you, to meet and get to know your brother Marines. Some guys I already knew from boot camp, like Reyna, a 5'7" husky but muscular Hispanic guy with a great sense of humor. Reyna was also a standout because of his physical toughness. He was from Idaho, and prior to joining the Corps, he was an accomplished mixed martial artist. Other guys I met for the very first time, such as Orozoco, a brother from El Paso, Texas. The guy was built like a tank and had a lot of balls. I remember one time Orozoco fought five salt dogs (senior Marines) at one time. Beltran was also from El Paso. He was a fun-loving guy who had turned down a track scholarship to become a Marine (later he would become a sniper under the call sign "Shadow 4"). We all became tight in SOI.

Once we were assigned squads, we were introduced to our instructors who would be our mentors. I got put with Sergeant Waters and Sergeant Castaneda. These men were squared away and knew their shit. They introduced themselves and immediately I liked them. When we were issued weapons, Sergeant Waters asked who wanted to shoot a machine gun. I raised my hand.

"Are you a hard charger, Martinez?" Sergeant Waters asked.

"I try to be, Sergeant."

"Having balls is all you need," he said.

He then handed me the M-249 Squad Automatic Weapon, better known as just the "SAW." The first thing I noticed was how much heavier it was compared to the M-16. After getting our other gear and additional lessons, we started our first field exercise and got initiated into the world of full-gear range runs. The one and a half miles at a steady pace wasn't so bad—it was the eighty to ninety pounds of gear you had to lug around that made things hard. But Sergeant Waters was an exceptional motivator. Above all else, he stressed the cardinal rule of Marine Corps doctrine. If somebody fell out of a run, he would make us run back and get the person. "Marines never leave Marines behind!" he would yell. Later, when many of us ended up in Iraq, it was a lesson we would live firsthand.

Sergeant Waters's leadership style was all about leading by example. During the month-long SOI, we spent days in the field and did physical training in our duce gear, the standard tactical gear Marines wore back then. But even then, the second we would stop training, Sergeant Waters would make us drop our gear and do a maximum set of pull-ups. Instead of dropping his gear, he'd keep it on and hop up on the bar and pump out pull-ups. "Motivate me!" he'd say. We would then yell motivating words as loud as we could while he would whip out with ease the more than twenty pull-ups you needed to get a good score on the physical fitness test. He didn't need our encouragement; the guy was an ox. But his leadership style got us directly involved in our leader's success and made us want to do our best. After all, we just saw him do more than twenty pull-ups *with* his gear.

Being part of the Marine Corps Rifle Squad also meant learning and living its mission statement. "What's the mission of the Marine Corps Rifle Squad?" Sergeant Waters would holler. We would shout back, "The mission of the Marine Corps Rifle Squad is to locate, close with, and destroy the enemy by fire and maneuver, or repel the enemy's assault by fire and close combat!" Still, even as we'd say the words, there was always that nagging question in the back of our minds about whether we'd ever get to live out our mission. I think that was one of the more mentally challenging parts of the training. You wondered and worried about whether you'd ever get to pop your combat cherry. But you trained with a warrior mentality anyhow.

Adding to the surreal nature of it all were the virtual reality training sessions where you were "inside" a video shooting gallery. It wasn't real, but I always tried to imagine that it was. I vividly remember one video simulation in which you found yourself in a Middle East desert setting. Terrorists would pop up out of nowhere and you had to engage them. In retrospect, it was pretty realistic. In one simulation, I killed the first couple of enemy shooters but was then eliminated, as more and more terrorists began multiplying on the screen. When I got killed, I stared at the screen and got pissed at myself for dying.

SOI threw a lot our way: assault courses, daytime and nighttime land navigation, MOUT (Military Operations on Urban Terrain) defense, offense and patrolling, and training with the M-16, M-249

SAW (squad automatic weapon), M-203, Claymore antipersonnel mines (aka claymores), M-67 fragmentation grenades, as well as old school hand-to-hand combat. The school ended with a final exercise, the mother of all training. During the most demanding portions, Sergeant Waters ran behind us and yelled, "Is this what you asked for?" "Yes, Sergeant!" we screamed back. "Then why the *fuck* are you dragging ass?"

Graduation from SOI concluded with the nerve-racking wait for what our military occupational specialties (MOS) would be. I wanted to be a 0311, which was a rifleman. Most of us did. But it wasn't up to us. I got what I wanted, but unfortunately some of my buddies didn't. Attention then turned to our unit assignment, which would determine where we'd live for the next four years. Nobody wanted to go to Camp Lejeune or 29 Palms. Both were in the middle of nowhere; Camp Pendleton and Hawaii were the locations of choice. Names and assignments were called out:

"Richardson, Victor, 1/6, Camp Lejeune."

"Felix-Barba, Victor, 1/6, Camp Lejeune."

"Reyna, Victor, 2/5, Camp Pendleton."

"Ray, Victor, 2/5, Camp Pendleton."

"Santiago, Victor, 2/5, Camp Pendleton."

"Martinez, Victor, 2/5, Camp Pendleton."

At least I'd be in the same unit with several of my tight friends. Enthusiastic handshakes were given. Little did we know, however, that something as simple as a roll call could, in a matter of seconds, cement our destinies. It had been a lottery of our lives, but in that moment, all we could think about was what kind of unit 2/5 was and where it was located. So I asked.

"Sergeant Waters, where is 2/5?"

"Up the road about three or four miles in Camp San Mateo."

"What can you tell me about 2/5, Sergeant?"

"It's the most decorated battalion in the United States Marine Corps. And that means that when you get there, you'll be hitting the ground running."

We graduated SOI days later, on November 10, 2000, the Marine Corps's birthday.

WHEN THE BUSES arrived to take us to San Mateo to join the fleet Marine force, 2/5 had sent the unit's biggest, tallest, most muscular Marines to pick us up. I didn't know where they got these guys, but they were the biggest sons of bitches I'd ever seen. Here we were, now about to become real Marines—no more games, no more bullshit—and this busload of giants rolls up ready to stomp us back down to size. *That settles it,* I thought, *I'm going to get my ass whooped.* But, if any of us had any illusions about transitioning smoothly into our new unit and companies, all that was shattered when our bus pulled up to the barracks. In fact, the scene turned into that of new joints arriving in prison. Every Marine stood on the catwalks of the barracks, hurling down obscenities at the top of their lungs, with promises of ass-whippings. That's when we were informed that we were no longer recruits or students but "boots," Marine lingo for new guys.

"Hey, boot! What you looking at?" one voice yelled.

"I'm going to fuck you up, boot!" another screamed.

"I'm going to trash you, boot!" a salt dog promised.

"Hey, boot! You better hope you're not in my platoon, boot!" yelled another.

As we got closer to the barracks, aka "the Red Roof Inn," so named because, well, it had a red roof, some Marines hurled soda cans and trash at us. It was a memorable housewarming party.

I was assigned Golf Company, 1st Platoon, 2nd Squad, 1st Fire

Team. Golf was a Helo company. Lance Corporal Allers would be my fire team leader. According to him, our fire team was shit hot. When we met our platoon's salt dogs, many of them let it be known that they hated boots. I sensed a theme.

I was put in a room with Egleston, a half-white, half-Mexican kid from Turloc, California. He was nicknamed "Itty Bitty" because of his 5'4" stature.

We got our gear and returned to our new rooms, all of which had been torn apart. The senior Marines then held a platoon formation on the catwalk and told us that if we didn't have our rooms cleaned by 4:00 A.M., we would all pay. Egleston and I made quick introductions and talked as we cleaned. When the conversation turned to our new senior Marines, we both agreed that we would have to stick together to make it through as boots.

That night, when Egleston and I hit the rack, we turned out the lights and what became known as 1st Platoon mentality was born.

"Good night, you fucking boot," I said. "Don't think that when you wake up you're salty just because you made it through your first night in the fleet, ass."

Egleston played along in a drawn-out voice like an unmotivated Marine, "A-y-e, l-a-n-c-e c-o-r-p-o-r-a-l."

"Are you being a smart-ass, boot?" I yelled.

"NO, SIR!" he yelled.

We both laughed and got some much-needed sleep—for an hour or two, that is. Senior Marines snuck into our rooms and gave us boots "blanket parties." Egleston and I had been asleep when we were awoken by six senior Marines in gas masks and ponchos.

"Good morning, Martinez! Fucking BOOT!"

Blurry-eyed and confused, I initially thought, *Am I dreaming this shit?* The salt dogs grabbed me, threw me on the ground, and kicked and punched the shit out of me. Another one grabbed

Egleston by the mouth and held him down. I fought back from the floor and even got in a couple good hits. But the Marines banging on me punched and kicked hard. Egleston, on the other hand, was more laid back and levelheaded. He just wrestled a little and sort of waited for the storm to pass. It was a great way to celebrate the Marine Corps's birthday.

I QUICKLY BECAME buddies with the other boots in 1st Platoon. There was, for instance, Collins, aka "Buku" (boocoo), a short, white kid from Oklahoma who was somewhat of a pretty boy and claimed that every girl he met liked him.

Another boot, Miranda, was a smooth operator from Louisiana. During his time in the Corps, he got into weight lifting and went through the sort of muscular metamorphosis you see in before-and-after shots in a fitness magazine.

There was also Magana, who was originally from Mexico but who had moved to Santa Ana, California, when he was nine years old. He joined the Corps at age twenty and was older than the rest of us boots. Little did I know then how much the two of us would go through together. Magana would become one of my closest friends.

Then there was Tardif, who would also become a good friend. At 5'11" and nearly 220 pounds, Tardif was insanely strong and supercompetitive and always went balls to the wall, which is probably why we got along so well. He was hardcore.

For example, in April 2001, we boots found ourselves training at 29 Palms (the most hated base of the Marine Corps) and embroiled in an ongoing battle with the salt dogs for supremacy. This often resulted in harsh TOPO (Tap Out or Pass Out) matches, which are a good way to relieve stress while taking out aggression on the salt dogs. The beatings got so bad, however, that we walked around paranoid that an ass-whooping could happen at any moment. One time we boots jumped Kim, an Asian-American salt dog, when the rest of the salt dogs were nowhere to be found. Tardif was the first to get Kim, grabbing him by the shoulders and literally throwing him through the air a few feet. Tardif wasn't mad; he was just playing around. But I remember thinking, *Shit, I'd hate to see him when he's pissed off.*

Then I did see him get pissed off. When the other salt dogs got wind of what was going on, they rushed to Kim's aid and it turned into a free-for-all. While I struggled with a 200-pound salt dog who was putting me in a choke hold, I caught sight of Tardif to my right. There he was, swinging three salt dogs around like rag dolls, their appendages flailing uncontrollably. The salt dogs tried to slow Tardif down by fish-hooking him and going for his nuts. But that didn't work; in fact, their attempts to cheat enraged Tardif in a way I'd never seen before. It wasn't the fighting that pissed him off; it was the lack of honor associated with fighting dirty. After five minutes of trying to subdue the enraged Tardif, the salt dogs wisely stopped the match.

I knew from the start that I liked this guy. The fact that he could kick ass one minute and crack jokes and laugh the next made him impossible *not* to like. But seeing what happened in the TOPO match with the salt dogs caused me to make a mental note: Never piss off Tardif.

Tardif's intense physicality was one of the things that made him a superb infantryman and leader. Not long after the TOPO match, we were out one night on the Helo Assault Course (HAC) in the bone-cracking cold desert. We were all bitching about the windchill factor being minus five degrees. But not Tardif. As he often said, "I love the pain." It wasn't macho bullshit; he seriously loved enduring maximum pain, including being frozen stiff in the damn arctic night air. Hell, when we were in the field, Tardif didn't even wear warming layers. I, on the other hand, did not love having my ass frozen solid. He was from Colorado; I was from New Mexico. I needed to take my mind off the frigid air and refocus my thinking. That could only mean one thing: Marine history story swapping.

"Hey, Tardif," I said in a low voice through chattering teeth.

"What up, Martinez?" Tardif said.

"Hey, man, this fucking sucks. Imagine the Marines in the Korean War and how cold it was for them. Shit, the gas for their vehicles even froze."

"I know."

"Tardif, got any stories?"

"Well, there's the one about a line unit in Korea who was on patrol in a whiteout [from the snow] and were surrounded by Chinese. Neither force could see because of the whiteout. The temperature kept dropping as night came. The visibility got so bad that Marines started getting separated from the patrol. So this one salt dog gets separated and gets so scared that he stops and prays, and after he's done, a man he doesn't recognize appears to his right in a Marine uniform. Knowing that the company recently got replacements, he asks the Marine his name. 'Michael,' the new guy replies. They try to find their patrol, but a few minutes later, the two Marines get ambushed by a Chinese machine-gun emplacement. The salt dog yells for Michael to get down, but instead Michael rushes the position and suddenly the loud volley of machine-gun fire falls silent."

"Well, did he die?" I asked.

"No," said Tardif. "The Chinese soldiers lay dead with sword wounds. Hearing the gunfire, the patrol finds the separated Marines. The lieutenant inspects the machine-gun nest, walks up to the salt dog, and says, 'Holy shit! Where did you get a sword from?'

'What sword?' the salt dog asks. 'A Marine named Michael is the one who killed the Chinese.' The lieutenant responds that they don't have any Marines with the first name Michael. The lieutenant just thinks the salt dog was being modest and chalks him up to being a hero. Later that night, the salt dog is getting ready to go to sleep when he reaches in his pocket and realizes something is missing. It was the St. Michael medallion his mother gave him before he went to Korea."

"So 'Michael' was St. Michael?" I asked.

"Yeah."

"That's cool."

"Your turn, Martinez."

"Okay, check this out. Gunny told me this one during a miserable field op. A Marine fighting in Korea got severely wounded on the face and neck during battle. When the smoke clears, his unit finds him and rushes him to the rear to get medical attention. There it's determined that the only reason the Marine hadn't died was because his wounds actually froze."

"Damn!" said Tardif.

"Yeah, but wait to hear the rest. So there were so many wounded that the corpsmen had to prioritize whom to treat first. A corpsman approaches the wounded Marine, who is still conscious because his wounds are stanched from being frozen. The doc checks his wounds, then hands the Marine a pen and paper. 'What's this for?' the wounded Marine asks. The corpsman looks him in the eye and says, 'There's a slim chance that you will make it through surgery. As soon as that wound thaws you're going to bleed out and die.' So the Marine writes a letter to his wife and children and gives his address to the doc. Minutes later, after getting on the operating table, sure enough, the wound thaws and he dies, despite the surgeons' attempts to save his life."

"Holy shit!" Tardif said.

"The Marine's death got put on 'hold' because it was so fucking cold."

After we traded Korean Marine stories, the windchill factor seemed not to bother me as much.

THE KING BADASS, the most intimidating man you could ever hope to meet, was a man we dubbed "Skeletor," First Sergeant J. K. Bell.

First Sergeant Bell stood a menacing 6'2" and had coal-black eyes, a face chiseled out of granite, and an impeccable uniform with gold jump wings and silver scuba mask. If you were to scribble in your head a caricature sketch of the stereotype of a kick-ass Marine, that's about what he looked like. He'd spent sixteen years in the direct-action platoon of 1st Force Reconnaissance, the USMC version of special forces. Everybody in the company thought he was a god. He radiated a glow of confidence and command, and it wasn't one achieved through fear so much as from intensity and ability. The man was a machine. On long hikes, for example, he'd hike faster backward than we did forward. It was embarrassing. Whenever he was around, and especially during inspections, the pucker factor was high. You were tight and on your game. Anytime he was near, I'd check my uniform over and over for any conceivable flaw that might invite his wrath. If a Marine had fucked up and gotten in trouble on, say, a weekend of liberty, it was not at all uncommon to see a Marine crying—*crying!*—as he left First Sergeant Bell's office.

One time, following Christmas leave, we all huddled to bullshit about what we'd done back home. Some guys told wild stories of getting drunk, while others amused us with tales of romps with chicks. There were always the usual—and increasingly redundant—crybaby sob stories about Suzy Rotten Crotch (Marine lingo for an unfaithful girlfriend) ditching them for some bagger at a grocery store or dipshit who worked at the food court at the mall back in Hometown, USA.

When it was Egleston's turn, we all thought he was going to recount some boring recruiter's assistant experience. Instead, he told us that the recruiter he'd assisted was with First Sergeant Bell when he was in 1st Force Reconnaissance. Every boot in 1st Platoon gathered around.

"You know how First Sergeant has tattoos on his legs?" he said. We all nodded.

"Well, I found out why First Sergeant has that snake on his leg." We leaned in.

"His nickname is Habu, as in the ultra-deadly Habu snake."

"Holy shit!" we all said in unison.

"Yeah, and the word is he is a legend in the reconnaissance community. Word is, he's every bit as hardcore as he looks."

We were acting like little kids who'd been given insider information about their favorite baseball player. But the guy was that charismatic. We later learned that First Sergeant Bell had been to just about every school a force reconnaissance operator could go to. When we attended the Marine Corps Ball, First Sergeant Bell's ribbons went all the way to his shoulder seam. It wasn't some myth. He was the real deal.

And it was for this reason that I made damn sure I was ready when inspections rolled around. Inspections were both visual and verbal. One of the things you could always count on, regardless of who was inspecting you, was that you'd have to field random questions. These questions were often designed to make you second-guess your Marine knowledge or to throw you off completely. The higher ranking your inspector, the higher the stakes. And so it was with the inspection we received from the commanding general, General Conway. We formed up in our Alphas and in strode the tall general. He had that friendly face that almost every general grade officer has. As he made his way through the ranks, he randomly selected Marines to talk with, after which his assistant inspector, who was a first sergeant, would inspect and grade their uniforms. That's when the towering general stopped in front of me.

"How do you like your unit?" he asked, peering down at me.

"I'm glad to be here with 2/5, sir," I said, staring at the center of his chest, looking at his impressive array of ribbons.

"Let me ask you something, son," he said. "What do you think about the chow hall?"

The chow hall? Did he say "chow hall"? My mind started thumbing through an invisible copy of the little green monster. I couldn't remember there being any section about what to say to a commanding general if ever asked about the quality of one's chow hall. So I went with something safe.

"I think it's a very good chow hall, sir."

"I see," he said. "And what do you like best about the chow hall?"

Best about it? Um, hmm . . . That we get to eat? I didn't want to sound like a smart-ass, but I honestly didn't know what he was looking for. I didn't want to mess up and say something stupid. So, instead, I messed up and said something stupid.

"I like the fact that you can get a cheeseburger every day if you want to, sir."

Unlimited cheeseburgers? Did I just really say that? Idiot!

General Conway burst out laughing. Thank God the man also had a sense of humor.

"Cheeseburgers, huh?" he chuckled. "Well, I'm glad you like it, son," he said. He then walked off and talked to another Marine as his first sergeant gave me an above-average inspection rating.

IN THE DAYS and weeks that followed, First Sergeant Bell exhibited hard Corps leadership and began the long, hard fleet buildup leading to our shove-off to Okinawa, Japan. But before we crossed the ocean or even hit the field, we would first need to draw weapons. I had yet to be issued my weapon and was hoping for a light M-16. Following SOI, I never wanted to see the hefty SAW again. The senior Marines who carried the SAW were happy to be getting rid of it. Who could blame them? They'd carried the cumbersome machine gun for more than a year and were eager to dump it on unsuspecting boots. When we got to the armory, Corporal Perez, a Mexican American salt dog squad leader, asked who wanted the SAW. No one volunteered.

"Nobody here's a hard dick?" he yelled.

More silence from all us limp dicks.

"Who carried the SAW in SOI?" he asked. There was silence. "Nobody, huh? O.K., then. Fuck it. Martinez. You got the SAW."

"Fuck. Why me, Corporal?" I protested.

"Because Mexicans are the only ones who can hack the SAW. Look. Magana isn't bitching."

I looked over at Magana. He didn't look too happy. As I recalled, he had told me he, too, hated the SAW. He had shown me a nasty wrist burn he'd gotten during his first field operation in Case Springs. He laid down so much suppressive fire that he had to change barrels and, in the process, the almost red-hot barrel had given him a nasty third-degree burn and a long scar to match. These were hardly the kinds of mementos you wanted from your first field operation.

"Trash" runs, grueling hikes, and field exercises and operations soon abounded. The pace of hikes was horrific compared to what we did in SOI. After one particularly difficult hike, a bunch of us ordered pizza. When the delivery guy knocked on the door, I looked at Egleston, he looked at me. "Fine!" he said. "I'll get it." He slumped off his bed and crawled on all fours to the door. He took the pizza from his knees as I crawled into the bathroom to wash my hands.

"Dude," the pizza guy said. "What happened to you guys? Every room I've delivered to has Marines that can't walk."

"Shit, man," Egleston said. "We just hiked twenty-six miles with a full combat load and few breaks in between." The delivery guy just looked at us like we were from another planet and shook his head.

During one brutal thirty-two-mile hike, we watched as one of our brothers, Salinas, an antitank assault man, fell out of the hike. He had had an aneurysm and was airlifted to a nearby civilian hospital. Days later, he died. Salinas's death hit the company hard. Anytime a brother dies, you feel it, both for the individual himself and for his family. Salinas loved being a Marine. He was hardcore. His death was something none of us ever forgot.

ON TRASH RUNS we'd run for miles and miles while singing different cadences. It's amazing how something as simple as sound and words can energize your muscles and focus your mind. I mean, nothing quite kicks your ass into high gear like hearing twenty guys singing:

> *A little yellow bird with a little yellow bill*
> *Was perched upon my motherfucking window sill*
> *I lured him in with a piece of fucking bread*

And then I smashed his little fucking head
Semper Fi, Do or Die.

But other, more serious cadences could motivate the hell out of you as you ran in formation, which looked cool. Every cadence caller had his own style; it's hard to beat straight-up classic boot camp running cadence. That's the type in which the sergeant calls it out line by line while you repeat after each sentence with the boom, boom of your boots keeping the rhythm. As we recited the words, I sometimes wondered if they'd ever apply to us.

If I die in a combat zone
Box me up and ship me home
Pin my medals upon my chest
Tell my mom I've done my best
Momma, Momma can't you see
Look what the Corps has done for me
Momma, Momma don't you cry
Marine Corps motto is Semper Fi

[change of caller]

Momma told Johnny not to go downtown
Heard the Marine recruiter was hangin' round
Johnny went downtown anyways
Wanted to hear what recruiter had to say
Recruiter asked Johnny what he wanted to be
Johnny said "I wanna be infantry"
Johnny caught a plane to Vietnam
There he fought the Viet-Cong
Many he killed by knife and blade

God only knows how many lives he saved
Well Johnny was bold and Johnny was brave
Johnny jumped on a hand grenade
Saved the lives of the men he led
But before he died this is what he said
"Momma, Momma, Momma please don't you cry
The Marine Corps motto is Semper Fi"

Cadence was only part of what built unity; my first field operations also gave me a chance to bond with my fellow boots and to get to know my salt dogs. We would do hours and hours of patrolling. At the end of the first night I got to know the members of our squad better. A squad leader had us introduce ourselves, after which he would ask us whether our mothers were MILFs (Mother I'd Like to Fuck). Some people entertained his question. I didn't.

After what seemed like hundreds of initial action (IA) drills, word was passed to clean rifles and hit the rack. While we cleaned rifles, the platoon bullshitted and found out a little bit more about one another. We were family now, and that was all that mattered.

That was also the night that Tardif started a tradition that would follow him the rest of his time in the Corps. When it was time to hit the rack, he yelled out as loud as he could, "Good night, Chesty Puller, wherever you are!" This brought on many ooh-rahs from the platoon.

STANDING ON fire watch at 3:00 A.M., holding my bulky SAW, I began to think back to home, friends, family, my car, and my old life. That all seemed so far away now, so distant. I took out my 7 Bravos (night-vision goggles, or NVGs) and stared through them, scanning the now lime-green terrain. Off in the distance stood 2nd

Platoon's fire watch. He looked deep in thought, too. With the brisk, cold wind hitting our faces, I wondered what had brought us all to the Corps. Where other branches promised money and short enlistments, we'd been promised pain. Something inside us had been drawn to that. I wondered why.

The next day I got in trouble when Corporal Perez found me more than an arm's length away from my rifle and snatched it. It was a stupid mistake on my part and I knew better. A Marine without his rifle is useless in war. Rifles were never to be out of reach—never. As an initial punishment, I was given three staggered hours of fire watch, which all but ensured no sleep.

That Friday, First Sergeant Bell had us form up to commend us on a job well done.

"Small-unit leadership, and knowing what your other Marines are doing at all times, are imperative to your survival in combat," he said. "Squad and fire team leaders must always know what every single Marine is doing when contact is called. IA drills, gents, will make you or break you during combat. Remember what I'm saying right now, and don't ever forget it."

He then turned it over to the commanding officer and the gunny, before setting us free for the weekend. The CO emphasized safety. Then the gunny had his turn. "No drinking and driving. No drugs. No arrests," he said. "Oh, and for all you new Marines, don't go to Oceanside to buy a car, especially not one from Liberty Motors. Dismissed." We shuffled back to our rooms like a gang of drunk geriatrics. We were sore and slow and tired—and it felt damn good.

BARRACKS LIFE at the "Red Roof Inn" in San Mateo was markedly better than boot camp. We were officially grunts in the fleet, so that counted for something. Still, the salt dogs were now our bigger brothers whose self-appointed job was to make us harder, tighter, and fleet worthy. One day you might be in their good graces, the next day, not so much. Their goal was to never let you grow complacent enough to begin believing that you'd "arrived," that you had earned the right to feel comfortable. And, even though salt dogs weren't formally tasked with sanctioning us, they had creative ways of "persuading" us to submit to being trashed when we screwed up.

All through SOI and field exercises and operations, I'd been gliding along, getting high ratings, praise from superiors, and even the occasional nod of encouragement from a salt dog or two. But that soon changed. In a matter of a few weeks, I went from being golden to a major shit bag who was viewed more as a platoon liability than an asset. Soon, I'd find myself at the bottom of a trench hole of my own digging—one I'd have to scrape and claw to get myself out of.

My decline was gradual. Having been more than an arm's length from my SAW on the last field op had not been forgotten, at least not by Perez. It was a Sunday night at the Red Roof Inn and we were all kicking it in my and Egleston's room when Perez coasted in.

"Boot, remember when you fucked up on that last field op?" he said with a shit-eating grin on his face. "I seem to recall that your weapon was out of your reach. Isn't that right?"

I knew he had something planned. I gave a quick neck-snap nod.

"So here's what we're going to do. You can either write an essay about the importance of gear accountability or you can trash. Your pick."

This really wasn't much of a choice. What he was really saying was, "Get up, you shitbird, and let's 'exercise' your mistakes out, you damn slacker!" But since it was stated as a choice, I didn't necessarily *have to* select the trash session. This, you see, made it all my decision. I didn't want to spend my weekend writing some bullshit essay, so I opted for the trash session.

"Good choice. Follow me," said Perez.

We walked into Magana's room. Perez opened the door to the head. Magana, Kelting, and Miranda were already inside trashing. Magana had apparently been a smart-ass to Kim. Kelting was a white kid from Minnesota. He had tons of freckles and reddish hair. Like me, Kelting had let his weapon get out of reach during the field op. Poor Miranda was getting trashed simply because he was in Magana and Kelting's fire team. And since the platoon was all about "fire team integrity," Miranda had been brought along for "moral support." Inside the head, Kim was the salt dog in charge of doing the trashing. I looked around the room and saw a series of "exercises" taking place. These workouts, however, couldn't be found on any fitness DVD or in a muscle magazine. These were *special* exercises.

Take, for example, Magana. When I walked into the head, he was in the "TV watching position." This is similar to a push-up position, only instead of supporting your torso with your arms and hands, you use your elbows and place the palms of your hands on your chin with your fingers going up the sides of your cheeks. You also have to keep your body straight while making sure that nothing except your toes and elbows touch the floor. The only time you're allowed to move is when you "change the channel." When this happens, you fully extend one of your arms and pretend to press an imaginary TV button while balancing your body on one elbow. Depending on the salt dog's mood, changing the channel can be quick or painfully long. The salt dog might ask you what you're watching on TV. If you say something he doesn't like, you have to change the channel. Any boot who makes a smart-ass comment like

"I'm watching an Olsen twins movie" is in for more sweating and quivering.

Across the room from Magana, Kelting and Miranda were in the "electric chair position." This involves sitting in an imaginary chair with your back against a wall. You do this until your legs burn and shake. Kim and Perez kindly offered me a seat in the electric chair. My fellow boots were drenched in sweat and shaking. For some strange reason that I've never understood, when you begin to hurt you start to giggle a little bit. The salt dogs knew this and would wait for the giggling to commence.

"Good," they'd say. "You think this is funny, do you?"

And that would be their cue to ratchet up the fun by putting you in a more painful position. Magana was among the first gigglers. His next exercise in our circuit training session was "monkey fuckers." To do a monkey fucker, you bend over at the waist, grab your ankles, and slam your butt down onto your heels before raising your butt back to waist level as fast as you can. Try it. See if that shit doesn't burn you out after five minutes at top speed.

Up next on Kelting's workout routine were "Smurf jacks." Smurf jacks require you to get down into a baseball catcher's position and do jumping jacks like a tiny Smurf.

I'd been in the electric chair for about eight minutes. My legs were shaking uncontrollably. I had dark sweat spots all over my green T-shirt. The bathroom mirror started to steam up, as our combined body heat had created a nice humid fog. I was then encouraged to watch some TV. Ten minutes later, Perez started my interrogation.

"So what are you watching, Martinez?" he asked.

"Um," I said, struggling to keep my balance. "*Revenge of the Nerds*?"

That, apparently, had been the wrong answer.

"Is that right?" he said. "So you want to be a smart-ass, huh? Good to go. Now you're going to do 'bouncing Bettys' in the toilet room."

Right then, "M&M," Mora Monroy, a Mexican kid who looked like an Aztec Indian and spoke softly and usually only in Spanish, walked into the main room. We were, after all, in his room, as he was Magana's roommate. It was piss-poor timing.

"Hey, M&M!" Perez said. "You came just in time for the party."

"But I didn't do anything wrong, Corporal," M&M whispered in broken English.

"Yeah, but Martinez did. So now you're going to trash, too. Look, we got all of Kim's fire team in here! Now we almost have a complete squad. And, you know the deal . . ."

"Fire team integrity," M&M muttered on cue.

"That's right!" Perez said.

By this time, I had been inside the head for about forty-five minutes. Magana and Kelting had been there at least an hour and ten minutes. Kelting was being a hard-ass and trying not to show pain, which was probably smart on his part, because if you did you'd only get trashed harder. I was in the toilet room and began doing bouncing Bettys. For this exercise, you squat as low as you can and then jump as high as you can. While you are airborne, you extend your arms, clap, and then yell "BOOM, BITCH!" as loud as you can. Ten minutes of bouncing Bettys went by and I was feeling the effects of the trash session. The mirror was covered with fog. It felt like a triple canopy jungle inside that head.

After about thirty more minutes of cycling through the positions, the trash session came to an end with Magana and Kelting in the electric chair, Miranda doing bouncing Bettys, M&M watching TV, and me doing monkey fuckers. We exited the head on rubber legs. It was great. We all laughed about how poor M&M had stepped into the shit by accident. The next day we went down to the armory to pull our weapons and prepare to depart for the weekly field op, an experience that would send me plunging straight to the bottom of the fleet heap.

A BOOT'S FALL from grace can happen in the blink of an eye and, often, over something that others might consider small but that salt dogs and superiors consider huge. About two-thirds of the way through our buildup in the fleet, I'd begun to fall ill. During the SOI final exercise back in October, we had been prevented from wearing warming layers in Camp Pendleton's frigid hills. Now, on the morning of this upcoming field op, I had woken up with something terrible and felt like roadkill. When I went to the armory to draw my weapon, the SAW felt unusually heavy. I told a salt dog in my squad that I wasn't feeling well and should probably go to the battalion aid station (BAS) to get checked out. He did what I probably would have done. He called me a pussy and said I should SITFU (suck it the fuck up). I knew better than to bitch and decided to go to the field sick as a dog.

This was going to be our first field op where we would be inserted into the field by helos. It was going to be an ass kicker, with long-range movements over one click (1,000 meters) at a time and through some of Camp Pendleton's most challenging terrain. The helicopters came on time, the ramps dropped, and I entered a helo for the first time. Corporal Perez took a headcount and gave a thumbs-up to the crew chief. Shortly thereafter, we were airborne with the wind rushing in as we quickly ascended to 13,000 feet. I looked out the window and down over the ocean. I could see the city of San Clemente. It looked beautiful sitting there on the ocean, with people splashing in the water and walking along the shore. I thought about how unaware they were, just as I had once been, of all the things that thousands of service members were going through and had been through to keep those beachheads safe and secure. They went along without a care in the world, which was just as we would have it.

Soon we were over the ocean and I got a little nervous. The city of Oceanside appeared on the right side of the helicopter. Oceanside is not nearly as nice as San Clemente. To tell you the truth, it's a fucking dump. Every Marine from Camp Pulgas on down had attached themselves to Oceanside. And with naïve young servicemen come conniving scum-of-the-earth leeches ready to take advantage of young Private Schmuckertelly. But that was neither here nor there. All I knew was that I was dog sick and the fun hadn't even begun.

We touched down and thirty minutes later during the tactical movement a corpsman approached me and asked if I was feeling okay. When I told him no, he gave me the Marine Corps remedy for every ailment: two 800 mg Motrin pills, or as jarheads call them, "Marine Corps M&M's." "Take two of these and drink plenty of water and you'll be fine," he said. Every corpsman in the infantry believes that you are malingering when you have something wrong with you in the field. Unless you were gushing blood from your eye sockets, corpsmen thought it was all a tactic to get out of rigorous field work. So when the young corpsman shot me the "yeah, sure you're sick" look, I decided it was pointless to try to explain.

We'd traversed two clicks over some rugged terrain and had stopped to begin setting up for the night. Staff Sergeant Semonic, our platoon sergeant, had decided that we would conduct an "admin bivouac," which meant that we would sleep in a platoon formation without a perimeter and only one fire watch. When I drew first fire watch, I thought my luck had begun to turn around.

First watch is the best watch to have, because then you can sleep the rest of the night undisturbed. But then, my luck took a turn for the worse. Corporal Perez took a weapons count to make sure we still had all our serialized gear. But as I walked over to grab my A-bag where my SAW's spare barrel was stored, my heart sank; the zippered pouch that housed my bayonet was unzipped and gaping open and yelling, "Yup, your shit is missing!"

I frantically rummaged through my A-bag, my MOLLE pack (Modular Lightweight Load Carrying Equipment), my assault pack, and my ass pack—no bayonet. My fellow boots helped me scour the area. Nothing. I finally informed my fire team leader, Lance Corporal Allers, who in turn reported to the squad leader, Corporal Perez. He had me look through my things again and retrace steps for the last one hundred meters. Still no bayonet. He then had no choice but to inform Staff Sergeant Semonic. The staff sergeant's fury cascaded down rank. First he chewed out Corporal Perez. Then Lance Corporal Allers. And then he laid into me.

"What the fuck is your problem, Martinez?" the staff sergeant yelled.

I snapped into parade rest for the ass-chewing.

"Nothing, Staff Sergeant."

"Then tell me, why the *fuck* did you fucking lose your goddamn bayonet?"

"I thought it was secure in my A-bag, Staff Sergeant."

"Do you have any idea where you might have lost it?"

"I think I might have lost it when we were moving through that dried-out riverbed."

"Fucking great, Martinez," he sighed. "You best square yourself away."

"Aye, Staff Sergeant."

"Now why the hell do you look like such a sorry piece of beat-up shit?"

"I've been feeling very ill, Staff Sergeant."

"Then why didn't you go to the BAS to get checked out?"

"I didn't want people to think that I was a pussy, Staff Sergeant."

Perez, who had called me a pussy back at the armory, glared at me in the moonlight.

Staff Sergeant Semonic calmed down a little and said, "First thing in the morning we're going back in that riverbed and looking for that bayonet. And God help you, Martinez, you better hope you find that motherfucker or else."

"Aye, Staff Sergeant."

The next morning, we looked for the bayonet in the riverbed to no avail. We patrolled several more clicks until nightfall. That night, we reached our destination and rechecked our gear. Everything except my bayonet was all there. The last thing I needed to do was lose another piece of gear. I grabbed my SAW and A-bag and went to use the bathroom. When I got back I noticed that my Kevlar helmet was gone. "Guys, that's not funny. Stop fucking with me. Who has my Kevlar?" They knew I was already a marked man because of the bayonet; this, I figured, was just them piling on and messing with me.

"Martinez, we're not fucking with you. No one took your Kevlar."

Son of a bitch! I thought to myself.

When I told Lance Corporal Allers my Kevlar was missing, I damn near thought he was going to have a stroke. When he told Corporal Perez, you'd have thought I had just told him I had murdered his entire family. Corporal Perez took me over to the staff sergeant to break the news in person. The staff sergeant's face flushed red. I thought he was going to beat my ass on sight. He had only five words for me: "Get out of my sight."

He commanded Corporal Perez to stay put. I hightailed my ass out of there. Running away, I could hear the staff sergeant ripping into Corporal Perez like a DI, all because of me. When Perez returned from his ass-chewing, I was now officially a shitbird. Another salt dog from our platoon ran up to me and grabbed me by my collar with both hands and jerked me forward. It was the classic 1960s geek-versus-jock high school bully scene.

"You fucking shitbird! What the fuck is your problem?"

My first instinct was to head-butt him in the nose, something that in my former life would have been automatic. But instead I tried to stay cool and speak calmly.

"You better let me go," I said.

"Or what, boot?" he sneered.

"Or me and you are going to throw hooks right here," I said.

I think the fact that I had the nerve to buck up to him surprised him a little, so he let me go. He huffed off to Corporal Perez and complained that I was a belligerent boot and that I should be charged. He wasn't an NCO and so had no such power, but since I was now a shitbag, he might as well have charged me.

As it turned out, the salt dog whom I'd almost thrown down with was in charge of making the fire watch list that night. Not surprisingly, he had me doing one hour on and one hour off fire watch through the night. I stubbornly refused my buddy Miranda's offer to take a few hours for me, but after my first two hours, I said, "Fuck it" and went to sleep. It was freezing cold outside. I was sick as a dog and tired as hell. So when I was awoken for my next watch, I got up, took a piss, and then hopped right back in my sleeping bag and fell asleep. It wasn't like this was actual combat, in which case I would never think of sleeping during fire watch. I almost pulled off my act of defiance when another salt dog spotted me getting out of my sleeping bag.

"What the fuck are you doing, Martinez?" he said. "Sleeping on watch?"

"Yeah, I'm sick," I replied.

"I'm telling Perez."

"Shit, go ahead!"

I was acting like the defiant shithead I'd once been. Sick or not sick, I had no right to act like an ass. But at this point, there was nothing that I couldn't fuck up. Everything I touched went to shit, the classic sign of a shitbag.

The next morning, the salt dog told Corporal Perez that I had shirked fire watch. This time, when Corporal Perez approached me, he did so with a tone and spirit of disappointment more than anger, something that cut far deeper than if he had just chewed me out.

"What the fuck happened to you, Martinez? You started off so good. You got an above average on your first inspection. You know your knowledge. What's going on? What's happened to you?"

"Corporal," I pleaded, "I'm sick. That's all."

"Martinez, I think I'm going to have to send you to 3rd Squad."

Corporal Longmire, a salt dog from 3rd Squad, overheard Corporal Perez's proposal and said, "Fuck no, Perez! I don't want that shitbag in my squad!"

Perez dropped the subject when Staff Sergeant Semonic walked up. When he learned of my outrageous behavior, he was all but speechless. To tell you the truth, I was lucky not to have been charged with dereliction of duty. He glared at me and said sternly, "Gunny wants to have a talk with you."

I walked over to the company command post (CP). That's when

Gunny let me know that I was the shitbird of all shitbirds and a blight on the Corps.

"Martinez, you are unsat [unsatisfactory] check," he said. "First you lose your bayonet. Then you lose your Kevlar. And then—then—you have the *audacity* to fall asleep on fire watch? What the fuck over? Oh yeah, that's right. What's this I hear about you being sick? You think that's an excuse to fuck up? Do you?"

"No, Gunny," I said.

"How do you plan to get that bayonet back?" he asked.

Of course, I had no answer.

"Now you can't even participate on this live fire range because you're going back to look for that bayonet. And if you don't find it, when we get back, the company won't go on leave, so I suggest you find it."

Holy shit! Make me run until my legs fall off. Dunk me under water. Hell, make me clean the damn head with my fucking tongue. But for the love of God, don't make me the reason the entire company can't go on leave!

"Do you understand me?" he snapped.

"Aye, Gunny."

"Now, if you can't find it, you'll have to pay several thousands of dollars to replace it, as well as that Kevlar."

Several thousands of dollars? I knew he wasn't fucking with me, because it seemed like every time we turned around, we were getting lectured about how expensive all our gear was and that that was one of the many reasons we best keep it in top shape. *Where the hell am I going to get several thousands of dollars to pay for high-quality military equipment?* I wondered.

"Martinez," he said, now inches from my sick face, "you better un-fuck yourself."

"Aye, Gunny."

A Humvee pulled up to take me to look for the bayonet and Kevlar. I had to borrow a helmet from one of the HQ Marines so I could ride in the Humvee.

After hours of looking for the proverbial needle in a haystack, we gave up and joined the company, which was now running the last platoon on the range. It happened to be my platoon. I stood alone in my platoon's area. As other platoons walked by, guys pointed and laughed. "Look at that shitbird!" one said. Word had spread like wildfire. Some Marines rained looks down on me with such scorn that I really thought they hated me.

A civilian watching might have said, "What's the big deal? Get another one. Move on!" But this was the Marine Corps way. If you fucked up, you became an example, an object of derision. Marines would go out of their way to not let you forget you fucked up. And you know what? That's exactly as it should be. You train for combat. There's no room for error in combat. A Kevlar helmet and a bayonet might be just "gear" on a field op, but in war, they could be the pieces of equipment that decide whether you or your brothers ride home in a box. I'd fucked up and been a bitch. And they had a responsibility to make me remember it so that it would never happen again. Over the next three years in the Corps, I never lost or misplaced another piece of gear.

When we got back to San Mateo and turned in our weapons, the CO let the company go on liberty but said that I had to replace the bayonet before the close of the next day (the day Christmas leave started). Otherwise, no Christmas leave for me. I had no idea how I'd find the same model in so little time. One of my fellow boots, Jaramillo, a half-Mexican, half-white kid from Santa Cruz, suggested that I go to downtown Oceanside and look around in the surplus shops. He even gave me a ride there in his Camaro. I walked into one store, Apollo's, headed to the counter, and started to describe what I was looking for.

"Lose a bayonet?" the store owner said with a smile.

"Yes, sir."

"I might be able to help you out. Is this what you're looking for?"

He pulled out the exact Vietnam-era bayonet I needed.

"How much?" I asked, bracing for his response.

"Twenty bucks."

"I'm sorry. Did you say twenty dollars?"

"Yeah, why? You wanna pay more?"

"Oh, no, sir. No. That sounds great. Yeah, I'll take it." I laughed. Either that guy was giving me the deal of the century or our Vietnam-era equipment wasn't worth "thousands of dollars" after all.

Back at the barracks, I dropped off my supposedly four-figure bayonet at the armory. As for the Kevlar, that night Dreyer, a cool guy from San Antonio, Texas, who had no love for salt dogs, had an extra Kevlar and was kind enough to give it to me, freeing me up to head home for Christmas leave.

When I got back to Las Cruces, I visited the medical officer over at the White Sands Missile Range. He said I had an advanced upper-respiratory infection and gave me pills and respiratory treatment.

"Why did you let the infection get that bad?" asked the doctor.

"Getting medical attention is viewed as a sign of weakness to us grunts," I said. "It's seen as malingering."

He scrunched his brow and gave me a confused look.

I spent the rest of leave beating myself up. I retraced the movements over and over again in my head, trying to figure out where I lost that piece of shit bayonet. But it didn't matter now; the damage had been done. I had "screwed the pooch," as we say in the Corps.

The bottom line was that my standing in the eyes of my superiors and brothers had been FUBAR (Fucked Up Beyond All Repair).

Rapelling, raid courses, the helo dunker, and live-fire ranges would be my redemption. I'd pass through each, regaining my footing in the fleet. Before long, I was tapped to be promoted to private first class. That's when I got my first taste of Marine Corps "pinning."

5

Far Eastbound

Ready?" the first salt dog asked.

I clenched my teeth, my jaw muscle pulsing.

"Ready?" he said again.

I nodded.

The prongs of my chevrons were hovering just below my collar-bone, suspended by the fabric of my shirt.

He balled his hand into a fist.

I clenched harder in anticipation.

He cocked back his hand-turned-hammer and let his hardest punch fly, right into my chevrons.

THUD!

When the metal prongs nailed into my chest, it sounded like a dropped melon hitting pavement.

The salt dog used his thumbs to rub the embedded chevrons before pounding the spikes deeper.

THUD!

I winced.

"You're not going to cry like a little bitch, are you, Martinez?" he said.

The second salt dog in line stepped forward and pried the prongs out of their new holes before mashing them back in again. This was followed by more thumb shifting of the chevrons, sliding them back and forth to stretch and deepen the holes in my skin. He then drove the barbs in with a powerful punch.

I was doing everything I could to control my facial muscles and hold back the grunts fighting to escape my mouth. My dad had told me about his "blood wings" experience following his graduation from Airborne school. He said it was a great tradition. I remember as a boy how cool and sacred it all sounded. When I'd asked if he got it bad during the "ceremony," he nodded yes. If one day I had a son, I thought, I wanted to be able to tell him the same thing regarding my first pinning ceremony. So I stood straight-faced and tried to look tough and unaffected.

"Oh, *look*!" the salt dog said condescendingly. "Martinez is trying to be a hard-ass." He rammed his elbow into my biceps, sending a wave of pain through my arms.

The third salt dog used his fingers like pliers and yanked the prongs from my skin. He made a third pair of holes and—back by popular demand—used his thumbs to slide the spikes around and expand the holes. When he punched the barbs in, I winced.

"Fucking bullshit!" he yelled. "I thought you were a hard-ass, Martinez!"

I walked back to my room, entered the head, and stood in front of the mirror to survey the damage. Honestly, it hurt more to pull the chevrons out than to have them pounded in. Bloodstains spotted my green undershirt. I took off my shirt, fingered the six bleeding puncture holes, and decided they needed cleansing. When the soap seeped down into the tiny flesh wells, it felt like six bees stinging my skin. When I went to reapply the chevrons and backings to my collar, I realized I'd need new chevrons. All the pounding and tugging had bent the prongs. For some reason this made me laugh.

In June of 2001 our plane took off from March Air Force Base in Riverside, California; 2/5 was heading to Okinawa, Japan, for the next six months.

When we landed in the morning, the salt dogs hooted and hollered, like a high school football team. To them, this was like losing their virginity all over again. When the door swung open, the Japanese humidity slapped us in the face. Even before all the moving and loading of buses, profuse sweating had already begun. Yet soon we were in our buses rolling to Camp Hansen, our new home.

Along the ride, the organic smells of Okinawa floated through the air. For the most part, the smell was sewage. Like I said, *organic*. The sights along the drive, however, were captivating. Tiny cars, bold colors, and unusual architecture—it was just as I'd envisioned it. When we finally pulled up to Camp Hansen, I was surprised to see the front gate manned by JPs (Japanese Police). About fifty yards behind the JPs was another checkpoint manned by a few Marines.

When we reached our barracks, Sergeant Washborne, our new platoon sergeant, announced that reveille would be at 0430 every morning and that we were not to go off base until we had the "Okinawa brief." Furthermore, he said, if we *were* caught off base, he would personally skull-fuck us.

The next week brought the mandatory and much-anticipated Okinawa briefing. The session was long and serious. High-ranking 3rd Division Marines spoke to us about the dangers of off-base liberty. They recounted past incidents that had given the overseas military a black eye. Rapes, other crimes, and egregious actions, they explained, had tainted our standing abroad. Indeed, certain military personnel, they claimed, were at that very moment locked away in Japanese prisons without a thing in the world the U.S. government could do about it.

And then they gave us the *really* important intel.

Once out in town, under no uncertain terms were we to buy prostitutes. The reasons given for this were many. The Japanese and Filipina hookers, it was explained, were unusually infested with rancid sexually transmitted diseases. In fact, some of these girls had STDs that were *so* bad that the diseases didn't even *exist* in the United States. If, for example, any of us were to contract the mysterious "Black Hand," we would not be allowed back into the United States and would be forced to spend the rest of our lives in Japan so as not to spread the "Black Hand" all across America.

Finally, because we were grunts, we were not to beat up any airmen or soldiers. Okinawa was one of the few places in which we would be in close proximity to the other branches. The volatile brew of, well, *brew* and different services could very easily lead to fighting. In other words, our superiors had us pegged and knew our kind all too well; grunts are notorious chest beaters and muscle flexers.

The briefing didn't keep us from roaming the island. The nearby town of Kinville was packed with bars. As soon as you'd walk into one of these establishments, a flock of shameless Japanese and Filipina girls would rush and cling to you. It was like an instant date. No sooner would you sit down with the girl than she'd start yapping, "Buy me drinkie. Buy me drinkie. Buy me drinkie." If you were sober, you'd usually have the sense to make the girls scram the second they descended on you. But if you were beyond a drunken haze, the girls could get increasingly better looking, and "Buy me drinkie" you might.

The annoying chick's order would be placed and the bartender would serve up a high-priced scotch glass full of Sprite. She'd quickly chug the Sprite. The girl would then resume. "Buy me drinkie. Buy me drinkie. Buy me drinkie." Another glass of Sprite, another fast chug, and soon you'd find yourself watching the worst acting job you've ever seen in your life. "I so drunkie. I so drunkie," they would say in fake slurred speech. If the drunk and horny Marine was stupid or drunk enough, he'd shell out more cash for the pricey fizz, all in the hope of getting laid. This, however, would not happen. And the dreaded "Black Hand" had nothing to do with it. The real reason young PFC Schmucktertelly wasn't getting any was that the girl was a shill for the house. She was there to run up tabs and drain wallets. She was the fly you swatted away but that always returned.

We spent a lot of time boozing in Kinville, Naha, and the gate 2 area. It got so bad, in fact, that our company was placed on mandatory Saturday-morning PT to stop us from drinking so much on Friday nights. I suspect all that partying was the result of our being in a pre–September 11 military that wasn't "getting some." *Getting some*—that's the Marine catchall phrase. It means everything: get some kills, get some action. *Get some!* Yet here we were in Japan, with no opportunity to "get some" in sight, so we tried to make the best of it and lived the fun, carefree overseas life of the pre-9/11 military.

Still, I saw the hunger, even desperation, for action. It was always swirling just beneath the surface, and you'd see it pop its head up from time to time. Even in jungle field operations we were excited but carefree. The salt dogs, on the other hand, made it seem like we were going into combat. Who could blame them? In the absence of war or any real combat, all they could do was rehearse and train. The salt dogs knew that for many of them, their time to be baptized by fire (combat) and become battle-tested Marines was quickly running out. They had to find something through which to live vicariously, an experience that allowed them to feel like their four years in the Corps wasn't just an exercise in marking time.

I had dreamed about jungle operations since I was a kid. The sounds of the jungle—the clicks of bugs, rustling of animals, and squawks of birds—were all just like in the Vietnam movies my friends and I had watched. Much of what we knew about the military we'd learned by watching and rewatching and memorizing these movies. Inside the jungle there was a constant hum emanating from somewhere you could never quite pinpoint. The musty, thick oxygen and humidity were intense. Light shone down through the treetops in certain places, and vegetation and crazy root formations sprawled across the jungle floor.

The farther into the heart of the jungle we got, the more we relied on land navigation skills. About one hundred meters into the jungle, it was like someone put the top up on a convertible; entering the triple canopy region of the jungle meant light barely pierced through the densely covered "roof" of trees. Our cammies were soaked in sweat, and we pounded water to try to cool off. We stepped as silently as we could and tried to avoid cracking twigs or rustling leaves. I ate the whole experience up—except for maybe when I saw a banana spider eight inches across (no kidding) crawling toward me.

The longer we shuffled through the jungle, the more I started thinking about all the men who served and fought in Vietnam. Those men lived, served, and fought in a damn jungle, where Mother Nature, not humans, reigned supreme. It reminded me of how spoiled and soft my generation was. Not that the jungles were now air-conditioned or anything, but the concerns we grunts had in the jungle—banana spiders and ants crawling on us, torrential downpours that made it impossible to sleep, and mongooses that ransacked our discarded MREs—were nothing compared to what

Vietnam vets endured. They worried about napalm burning their flesh off and Charlie putting rounds in their bodies, and here I was complaining about ant bites, spiders, rain, sleeping in mud, and a fuzzy little mongoose?

Sometimes I don't think our generation gets it. Sometimes I think because we have the Internet we think we've "been" everywhere and "experienced" everything. Bullshit. Spending weeks in the jungle taught me more about Vietnam than any textbook or website ever could. It taught me to shut my ungrateful mouth and remember that our Vietnam fathers fought and lived through hell, only to then come home and be kicked in the teeth by disrespectful, spoiled rotten, antimilitary hippie jerk-offs.

That wasn't all the jungle taught me. While the temptation was always to see these operations as "just exercises," I understand in retrospect how invaluable they were in terms of preparing us for combat—what all the salt dogs were itching to get into. During a graded helo raid on a jungle base, I rushed a machine-gun bunker and "killed" the enemy, "destroyed" the bunker, and proceeded to get myself "killed." Sergeant Washborne had to carry me back to the extraction site. During the debrief, the LT announced that he was impressed with the raid and that I had done an excellent job rushing the bunker.

"Sir, if I died, didn't I fuck up?" I asked.

"No," he said. "Because of your actions, only *you* died, instead of the platoon. You sacrificed yourself so that others could complete the mission. If you had not done what you did, we might have failed the raid."

AFTER A FEW MONTHS in Okinawa, we were all ready for a change. I had been promoted to lance corporal, but I had also been assigned to mess duty—a most hated duty that meant rising each morning at 0400.

One night, I hit the rack early and fell quickly into a deep sleep.

Next thing I knew, Kelting, my roommate, was standing over me.

"Wake up," he said. "A plane struck one of the Twin Towers in New York."

"It's probably just a drunk-ass pilot in a small Cessna," I replied in a groggy voice.

I rolled over and went back to sleep.

6

Pray for War

Kelting walked back in minutes later.

"Martinez, wake up," he said. "A second plane hit the second tower."

Still half asleep, I sat up in bed.

"Two huge passenger jets crashed into the towers," said Kelting. The words "passenger jets" sent a jolt through me.

"What?" I said.

I jumped out of my rack and followed Kelting to the beat-up recreation room where rows of silent Marines were all staring at the television. When we got there, the Twin Towers were still standing and pluming smoke. Every American remembers the images: the falling bodies, the terror-struck faces, the New York police and firefighters—the true heroes of 9/11—racing *toward,* not away from, the inferno.

With each new image beamed across the ocean, the worry within my soul magnified. Watching events unfold, I was at once transfixed and revolted. I had to pull myself away from the television to get to the chow hall in time for mess duty. The million thoughts that raced through your head raced through mine. Who or what was responsible for this?

When I got to the mess hall, I watched the big screen and tried to muster an appetite. It was no use. And it was there, sitting in a chow hall in Okinawa, Japan, that I saw the scene that would change the world. Those grand, beautiful, strong structures collapsed. The chow hall went silent. "My mom works there," I heard a brother Marine say to no one in particular.

"My father works in the city," another said.

That was all I could take.

I got up and headed for the door. A cook tried to stop me.

"What do you think you're doing?" said one of the cooks, knowing I was supposed to be on mess duty. "You still have work to do."

"I signed up for the grunts, not to be a cook," I said.

I ran toward the barracks, where only hours later we had a formation. First Sergeant Bell said that America had suffered a devastating terrorist attack and that the base was on lockdown; there would be no more liberty. Our steel-forged first sergeant explained that we would board the ships early and begin preparing for combat.

This is where the road divides between those who wear the uniform and civilians. This is where what I'm about to say will either make you nod knowingly or shake your head in confusion, maybe even revulsion: The Marines of 2/5—myself most assuredly included—began cheering and smiling and high-fiving and celebrating.

Here's why: We were the ones who were going to get the privilege of doing something about the hell that was on your television screen. We felt honored, privileged, God-blessed—and ready to rip the motherfucking face off the enemy.

You go infantry for one reason: to defend our great nation. When we cheered, it wasn't the foolishness of youth or a lust for violence like antimilitary nitwits would have you believe. (For people who think they're so much smarter than everyone, they don't know or understand shit.) Our enthusiasm wasn't about revenge. No, it was about letting dads hug their kids. It was about letting mothers tend the tears of children. It was about letting you get back to doing whatever it is you do, secure in the knowledge that tens of thousands of surly, violent, precision killers like us stood ready to do the dirty work of defending democracy. "Don't worry," our jubilation was saying, "we got you covered, America. Go home. Go to sleep. Go to work. Go to church. Live. Pray. Love your babies. Don't even think about the hell you've seen. Erase it from your mind. Consider it handled. We got your back. It's all on us. Thank you. Thank you for the privilege. Thank you for the honor of defending you and everything we love. Don't worry. Go in peace. We're on it."

It's a mentality that only those who share it can understand. If you've ever worn the uniform, you do.

We were eager to become real grunts and men. As a boy, the call to arms whispered in my ear. In high school that whisper became a shout. Now the call to arms had become a roar. It was a destiny and a moment I had played in my head a hundred times before—the moment when I would be baptized by fire. The attacks on our country would not go unanswered, and that simple fact elevated the intensity of everything we did. From that day forward, things would change. I barely drank alcohol at all, though I had been a major league partier along with the rest of the Marines. Daily workouts were no longer about building our physiques or getting girls. Hitting the gym was now about endurance and outlasting the enemy. Everything became purposeful. And real. Training wasn't about machismo or outperforming a buddy. No, strength now held battle-field implications.

On 9/11, the seriousness of the situation quickly consumed us. At the armory, we did not speak during weapons cleaning. Missing gear, usually a hassle to get replaced, was reissued with no trouble. Whatever you were missing you got. No questions, no problems. We were then let off to call home. Lines were long and phone lines were jammed. We, like everyone, got a busy signal.

Nightfall closed out the most devastating attack on American soil in our nation's history. Marines are hardly aces at sensitivity or empathy, but we did our best to be there for one another. I walked around the barracks, room to room, visiting with buddies. Conversations spanned the map, everything from the importance of family to mortality to terrorism to combat. We were especially mindful of guys with family or friends who might have been in harm's way. But each grunt had his own way of sifting through it all. And I had mine.

I returned to my room and looked around for Kelting. He was in another room. I didn't want him or anyone else to see what I was about to do. I got down on my knees and took a deep breath. It had been a while. I tried to empty myself of the rage inside. I clasped my hands together and began to pray. I asked God to keep my family safe. I prayed for the people in New York. I asked God for forgiveness for my sins and for not using the body He gave me for His purposes. And then I prayed for war. I asked that if war were to come that my unit be sent into combat. I asked for justice. I asked that He would give me decisive action against sworn enemies of the United States. I ended my prayer by asking that God did with me whatever He wanted to.

Word was passed that, due to the events of 9/11, the ships USS *Belleau Wood*, USS *Juneau*, and USS *Essex* (31st Marine Expeditionary Unit) were leaving Sasebo in mainland Japan and would pick us up two weeks earlier than previously scheduled. We were headed to Afghanistan.

When the time came, we were bussed to the docks to load the ships, which looked like massive floating steel fortresses. During our formation on the *Essex*'s flight deck, we were informed that this was the home of sailors and that we were to treat the facilities and individuals as such. Translation: "Don't fuck with the sailors." The corpsmen were especially happy, since they were around their fellow Navy personnel. They were now back on "the blue side," among Navy, instead of their usual plight of being stuck tending to Marines' medical needs.

We walked in a straight line to find our berthing area. Many sailors were understandably unhappy that we were now aboard. More people meant longer lines for chow and more personalities to deal with. The ship's enormity, however, kept most of us relatively humble; I would have gotten lost if I was not following somebody who knew where he was going. At the berthing we turned in our weapons to our armory and set up shop.

I got seasick the first week on the ship. In our berthing area, I ran to the bathroom and threw up violently until I was dry heaving. Kneeling on the floor, hating life, I suddenly realized I wasn't alone. I heard a volley of other Marines blowing guts, too. I started laughing like a madman. I couldn't stop laughing. I drank more water from my canteen only to then instantly spew it up again. I was still laughing. *What a bunch of killers!* I thought to myself. *We can't even keep our chow down on fucking ship!*

I'm sure the sailors all got a big charge out of seeing some of us dick-swinging grunts puking like little bitches.

The biggest adjustment to ship life was getting used to sleeping in the racks. They were more like coffins than beds. Ship racks are stacked on top of one another, leaving little more than a foot of open space to move around in or to sit up. I got stuck with a bottom rack, and every morning, without fail, I'd wake up and bang my head on the bed frame above mine like a jackass.

Days on the ship were spent PTing in the gym during Marine hours, studying knowledge, and disabling our weapons for time both with and without being blindfolded. We were getting ready to go to war. First Sergeant Bell ran practice raids and administered a class on the Rules of Engagement (ROE). Listening to all the "dos and don'ts" of the ROE was a real eye-opener for many of us. They were superstrict. It almost felt like the enemy could get away with virtually anything he wanted while we would be under the glare of an international microscope. At one point, out of near exasperation, someone finally said, "First Sergeant, what if they're pointing their weapons at us?" Despite his imposing and intimidating presence, First Sergeant Bell had a great dry sense of humor. He wryly delivered the perfect response. "That's easy. In that case, we're going to give them a couple of 'love taps,'" he said. Everyone sort of looked at one another. No one said anything, for fear of the mighty Skeletor. Then the first sergeant cracked a grin and the whole classroom erupted in laughter. The loose translation of his words being "We'll shoot them."

But then the hammer dropped on us: It was announced that we would not be going to Afghanistan as planned. The 1/1 Marines, not the 2/5 Marines, would exact America's revenge. Morale plunged. Sure, we were told our first liberty port would be the beach town of Darwin, Australia, a place few kids from New Mexico would ever experience. But I hadn't joined the Corps to hit liberty ports during a time of war. We were now a unit without a mission. Everyone around us was "getting some" except for us. With each passing day, it seemed less and less likely that we would *ever* get some. In our four-day stay in Australia, some other boots and I had to pull duty in the well deck of the ship where all the tactical vehicles were housed. I walked around all the tactical vehicles and weaponry thinking what a waste of firepower this was, with no terrorists in sight to decimate.

In Australia, our platoon decided to drown our frustrations at a place called the Coyote Cantina. Corporal Perez got the squad together for a dinner, where our squad did what drunk grunts do: profess their willingness to die for one another.

We bought a bottle of Patron and took shots. Before slinging back every shot of tequila, each of us took turns making a toast with our own personal statement to the terrorists. "On behalf of all Americans," Tardif said to the invisible terrorists, "I'm going to kill you motherfuckers." A burst of ooh-rahs rang out.

Magana was up next. Magana, the elder of our group (he was all of twenty-one years old), had a laid-back but lethal edge to him. He also had a dry sense of humor, so I knew his toast would have some funny smart-ass twist to it. He didn't disappoint. With shot glass raised, Magana said, "Terrorists, I have just one thing to say: I'm going to kill you good." We all burst out laughing.

After a few more toasts, my turn rolled around. I wasn't in a comedic mood.

"The truth is, I just don't give a fuck about dying," I said.

Everyone got quiet.

"Shit, these punk-ass motherfuckers think they can fuck with my country and I'm going to just let that shit ride? Fuck that! I'm getting me some 'get back.' If I die, I die."

I'd broken the upbeat mood. I felt civilian eyes staring at me from the bar.

"And if I die, bros, I'm taking all kinds of motherfuckers with me!" I yelled through my slurred speech. "And you know why?"

Tardif shot up out of his chair. He had that same demonic look in his eye as he'd had back at 29 Palms months ago when fighting salt dogs. He slammed his hands down on the table.

"WHY?" Tardif hollered.

"Because I'm a MOTHERFUCKING UNITED STATES MARINE!" I thundered.

Tardif hunched over in a muscle-flexing pose and let out a savage yell.

"FUCK YEAH!"

Our entire table sprang up and howled like rowdy football fans during a touchdown. I'd officially incited a drunken, riotous, obnoxious rage. But what the hell? We were drunk ($400 liquor bill). We were Marines. And we were twenty-somethings headed for war.

While my theatrics were alcohol-induced, I meant every word of what I'd said. My words, I later found out, had stuck with Tardif. On New Year's Eve, Tardif brought up my Australia oration.

"Hey, bro. Did you really mean what you said in Australia?" he asked.

"Yes. Why?" I said.

"Because a lot of guys say shit like that. They say they're ready to go savage. But I could tell you were serious."

"I was. I want to go toe-to-toe with these fucking cocksuckers, Tardif. I mean it."

"Me, too."

His voice and face let me know he meant it just as much as I did.

When we shoved off from Australia, we headed off to conduct a humanitarian mission in East Timor. It wasn't combat. But at least it was real-world stuff, which made everyone perk up a little. Sections of the company took off from the flight line aboard CH-46s to head toward the East Timor coast. Most of my platoon remained aboard the ship, since we were a reaction force designed to respond in case shit hit the fan. When it never did, our reaction force, named Sparrow Hawk, became known as "Sleepy Hawk," because nothing ever happened.

Upon leaving East Timor, we crossed the Equator, triggering something called "WOG Day." WOG Day is authorized hazing that celebrates a "pollywog's" (person who hasn't crossed the Equator) transformation into a "shellback" (a person who has). Each WOG had to give one green T-shirt to a shellback, who scrawled words and pictures on it about the WOG in order to embarrass him. When I got mine back, one enterprising salt dog had written in big bold letters across the front: 1ST SGT BELL CAN'T TRASH ME.

Oh great! I thought. If First Sergeant Bell saw that, I was definitely fucked.

WOG Day was an all-day trash session. We were made to enter the shower fully clothed, were hosed down, and had baking flour thrown on us. Then we were trashed some more. The Navy shellbacks fucked with us hard. We had to do what they said, otherwise we wouldn't get the mandatory meal that one must eat in order to become an official shellback. The meal? Disgusting green eggs and ham and a dollop of blue oatmeal. Under the flight deck, the trashing got harder and we were hosed down again. We WOGs were made to blow the water that filled up the "cat eyes" (holes on a deck for chaining things down), which winded us because the holes filled right back up with all the hosing.

And then First Sergeant Bell spotted my T-shirt. He trashed the shit out of me DI style. But he and everyone else thought the shirt was hilarious. Me, not so much. After that, the WOGs finally made it to the flight deck, where we waited in line to be judged by "King Neptune," who would determine whether we were worthy of becoming shellbacks. We sat in two long lines half the size of the flight deck and were continuously hosed down. When I made it to the front, King Neptune made me lie on my stomach and do circles in a small plastic kid's pool while yelling, "I'm a mighty, mighty shell-back!" I'd rather have had to hike twenty miles than do that shit.

After forty-five days at sea, we finally returned to Okinawa, having seen no action. No one knew for sure how long we'd be back in familiar Japan, since deployment schedules were mixed up. Soon it was back to business as usual, complete with field ops, trash runs, and hikes. But the fact that the War on Terror was being waged somewhere and that we weren't part of it weighed heavily on us.

One night, I came back from working out and eating with Magana. The room was dark and I started to undress and get ready for bed. After brushing my teeth, I looked over at Kelting's empty rack before lying down in my own. I closed my eyes and was just about to fall asleep when a voice startled me.

"We're never going to 'get some,' Martinez."

I wrenched my neck around toward the voice. There in a darkened corner sat Kelting with a bottle of Gentleman's Jack.

"What are you doing in the dark, Kelting?" I asked.

"We're never going to 'get some,'" he repeated. "You know that, right?"

"Kelting, what are you talking about?"

He felt as low as we all did. We weren't getting some. Others were. The truth is that a Marine, especially a grunt, can begin to feel really inadequate when he knows a unit other than his is engaged in combat. I know I felt that way. Being a grunt is really the only MOS (military occupational specialty) for which you train solely for what you *might* do as opposed to what you *will* do. But a grunt only gets to go through hell (combat) a few times—or sometimes never at all. He'll either stay in until he gets some or leave the Corps blue-balled

and unfulfilled. It might sound strange, but this type of disappointment was the kind of thing that could stay with a guy for the rest of
his life. Some of us were beginning to fear we might never get some.

"We were in the right place. We were ready. What happened?"
Kelting said.

"Shit, man. First Marines were closer. We just had bad luck.
Maybe we'll get to go after we get back to California," I said, knowing full well what I was saying was bullshit.

"Fuck that," said Kelting. "Our time has passed, Martinez.
We're all going to have the four-year itch."

He'd been man enough to express what a lot of us were thinking
but were too afraid to say aloud. I convinced Kelting to get some
sleep. After all, the next morning we had to clean weapons that
would never see combat.

BEFORE WE LEFT OKI, we had to complete a tradition that I hope
still goes on. In the ceiling of each room in the Oki barracks is a
trapdoor that opens up for extra storage. However, no one uses it for
that purpose. Instead, it's used for passing on something to the unit
relieving you. Most Marines left hardcore pornography, since it's illegal in Japan (or at least that's what the Corps enforces). When I
first checked the trapdoor in my room, I found a list of the best bars
and clubs to go to, a small electric fan, and some jungle boots. I decided to leave a nice pair of khakis and a short-sleeve black polo
shirt. It's almost impossible to find cool things to wear in Oki. And
if you do, everybody else has the same thing because they bought it
at the PX. I hoped the new owner of the pants and polo shirt would
have as many good times on "The Rock" as I did. I closed the trapdoor. My deployment was over.

In the months that followed, we, like the rest of the nation, waited for the commander in chief to make his move. The drumbeat of war passed from Afghanistan to Iraq. But to us it seemed like forever. I trained. And waited. I bought a Camaro. And waited. I was promoted to corporal and got my "blood stripes." And waited some more. It was excruciating. But no more excruciating than it must have been for our senior Marines leaving the Corps with the four-year itch (no combat).

When the last salt dog left, it reminded me that we were now on our own. I hoped I was ready to lead men into combat.

One thing along the way that helped get our minds off waiting was getting our own "boots." We were salt dogs now, and we got all the privileges that came with it. I had always told myself that when I became a salt dog, I wouldn't randomly haze my boots. I'd hated it when my seniors fucked with me and was determined to chart a new course. But, like a boy who watches his alcoholic father only to make and then break his vow to be different, I, too, ended up hazing my fire team. Not as bad as we got it, but we hazed them nonetheless, like the time we made them walk the gauntlet. We got Birdsong, Gardner, Jones, Lott, McCall, Miguel, O'Brien, Pflueger, Rivias, Siler, Terrone, Voller, and Welsand. My fire team consisted of Garcia (a senior Marine), Miguel, Birdsong, and Terrone. I liked them all right from the start.

Our boots were all post-9/11 Marines, an honorable breed to be sure. During one field operation, the platoon sat in a circle and each person explained why he joined the Corps. When salt dogs spoke, the answers were what you might expect. Some people spoke of honor. Other guys said it was to find adventure. And still others said it was to serve their country. But the boots' answers were different. The words they used to describe their motivations included "September 11," "terrorists," "anger and revenge," and "justice." Not a single person sitting there said "money for college." In fact, some of the boots in the circle were older than most of us salt dogs and dropped everything to serve. O'Brien and Terrone, for example, were from New York. O'Brien, a smart white guy from Buffalo, was almost done with a degree. And Terrone, a 5'8" Italian who never met a Frank Sinatra song he didn't like, had left behind the chance to take over his family's business. Terrone said that the recruiting office near Times Square had been jammed when he found his calling.

I was proud of the boots. They were as ready and eager to get some as we were. In infantry, that's all you can ask for. They, like every American, knew war was imminent. And they joined anyway. Better yet, that's *why* they joined. We salt dogs respected that. Our boots were hardcore from the start.

DURING OUR LAST evaluation of simulated urban combat, held in Victorville, California, after a buildup that lasted more than a year, I was shot dead in the middle of a street. Lying on my back and looking up at the sky, I started thinking about how if this had been real, the sky would have been the last thing I saw.

As I lay there on the ground, my mind floated back to an experience Magana and I had shared several months earlier that convinced me I would forever see the world through Marine—not civilian—eyes. In July 2002, while on liberty, Magana and I decided to drive to East Los Angeles for a night at a hot spot called QC's 20/20. We sat at the bar kicking back drinks and looking at pretty girls. And that's when I realized that Marine culture had permanently changed me. I overheard the frivolous conversations around us—pointless chatter about meaningless things.

I nudged Magana.

"What's up?" he said.

"Hey, man, do you realize that all these people in here are fucking clueless?" I said.

"What do you mean?"

"I'm serious. None of them have a worry in the world."

We scanned the smiling, dancing Los Angeles mass on the dance floor.

"Do you think any of them are going to Iraq like us to get their asses blown off?" I said.

"Shit, man," said Magana, "I can't *wait* to go out there and fucking get some. Ever since Oki I've been waiting for my chance. It's the chance to finally scratch the itch, you know?"

"Yeah, I know. Believe me, I know. I've been ready for this shit since I was four years old. I hear you. All I'm saying is that this—all this around us—this isn't real."

"What do you mean?"

I sighed. "This life, civilian life, isn't the real world. These people are living a Candy Land existence, bro. They don't have to worry about the shit we have to worry about. I'm not complaining. That's the way it should be. But we take care of all the crap so they can live like this and not worry about dying and all the terrorists trying to destroy our country. But guys like us—twenty-one and twenty-two years old—carry the shit bucket so that they don't have to."

We looked back out over the crowd of L.A. clubgoers.

"Are you ready to die, Martinez?"

"Yeah. You?"

"If I have to, yeah."

Right then, some girls walked up and wanted to dance. We declined and kept talking.

The sound of gunfire jolted me from my mental movie of my and Magana's dance club epiphany. It brought me back to the field op. I looked away from the clouds and saw many more Marines lying "dead" on the ground. This was as real as it got. None of us were taking this training lightly. Since joining the Corps, I'd been told that during urban combat, a rifle company could sustain 80 percent casualties. Until the field operations, I'd brushed that statistic off with a "Yeah, right." But after a few raids and assaults, I knew the numbers didn't lie.

After that last field op, we were granted thirty days' leave. "Enjoy your leave," we were told, "because when you return, you'll be deploying to the sandbox [Middle East]." I drove my black Camaro the eight hours to New Mexico. When I told my family and girlfriend I'd be heading to the Middle East, they responded with mixed emotions. Most Americans by that time had come to terms with the fact that we were going to war in Iraq. It wasn't a question of if, but when. So my parents took the news as well as could be expected. Being a military family, they understood. My girlfriend, on the other hand, didn't take it as well. Before long, she began complaining about how lonely she'd be while I was gone and how hard it was going to be on her while I was off fighting a war. Her self-absorption bothered me on many levels.

While on leave, I decided to pay a visit to the local VFW. I wanted to ask the old warriors if they had any advice for me before going off to war. We all sat together at a big table. As I listened to the old men speak, I studied their ribbon-covered hats. Each had words embroidered across the face—words like "Vietnam," "Korea," "Tet '67," "Pusan," "Guadalcanal," and "Iwo Jima." Each man recounted stories of hope and hell. I was among men who knew far more about what I was about to experience than I did. They were gracious and wise. I liked them. I listened.

One of the things I had heard from many veterans was that a warrior needed to have a clear mind in war. So I did myself and my fellow Marines a favor. Having heard stories of men who in past wars had been preoccupied with thoughts of girlfriends instead of battle, I decided to DTB (Marine lingo for "dump that bitch") and focus my body, mind, and spirit on what lay ahead. When I told the old warriors of my decision, they nodded approvingly. Before I got up to leave, they gave me parting advice: "Your rifle is everything. Keep your bayonet sharp. Keep faith in God." I thanked them for their time, wisdom, and service. When I returned, they said, I was welcome to join their chapter.

Over the next several days, I felt more alone and more alive than ever before. The simplest things took on new depths of meaning and brought greater joy. I'd lived in New Mexico for thirteen years, but I'd never taken the time to appreciate the physical beauty of the mountainous terrain and landscape. So, every morning and night, I climbed up A-Mountain, a peak in Las Cruces that locals climb once a year to repent of their sins. I, on the other hand, climbed it to soak in the breathtaking New Mexico sunrises and sunsets (a quick dash up a mountain seemed too small a price to cover all my past sins). Looking out over the expanse, I replayed the scenes of my life like a movie in my mind. I realized that America and my family meant more to me than I'd ever understood. The grandeur of the vistas humbled me, and I felt more tranquil and grateful than I'd ever felt before.

Before leave ended, I had a few other things I wanted and needed to do. One of them was to buy a large knife, which every Marine should have. My father and I took a day trip to El Paso, Texas, and enjoyed each other's company while hunting for the perfect knife. After failing to find one, we tried a knife shop in Las Cruces and immediately I spotted the knife I'd been looking for. It was a huge KA-BAR with a leather sheath. The store owner took the knife out of the case and put it in my hand. It felt perfect. I slashed the air using different stabbing motions we'd been taught during Marine Corps martial arts instruction. I guess it must have looked a little too intense.

"You going to kill somebody with that?" the owner asked jokingly.

Not really thinking, I said, "Hell yes."

The owner looked disturbed.

I clarified.

"I'm a Marine. I'm going to Iraq."

"Oh, man," he said. "Now I get it. Tell you what. Since you're protecting our country, I want to give you a thirty percent discount."

"Thank you, sir."

"No. Thank you for your service."

My father said he wanted to be the one to buy my knife. I thanked him for the gift as the patriotic owner rang us up. As we walked out of the store, the clerk said, "May that knife serve you well, Marine." I was grateful for his generosity.

When leave was finally up, my parents honored my wishes by not giving me a teary-eyed good-bye. They knew I'd hate that, so they tried to hold back the emotions and told me that I was loved and prayed for.

When we all reunited at the barracks in Pendleton, we attended a battalion meeting where it was explained that we all needed to make out our wills. Writing a will at the age of twenty-one is a sobering experience. What I had I gave to my parents, but like most Marines, my only possession of any value was my car. I'm not sure which was odder—creating a will or imagining my mother riding on twenty-inch wheels with the top down.

There was one more order of business: I drove to Los Angeles to get a tattoo. Magana came with me to get a huge Aztec tribal tattoo on his back that spanned shoulder to shoulder. I was looking for something that said I was a Marine but that wasn't the traditional USMC; Eagle, Globe, and Anchor; or bulldog wearing a Smokey Bear. Then it hit me: DEATH BEFORE DISHONOR. It was an old-school Marine saying that the mainstream public was almost entirely unaware of. I told the tattoo artist I wanted it on the upper part of my back, above my shoulders and just under my neck.

When I took off my shirt, my large gang tattoo drew a double take from a few people inside the shop. The new Marine tattoo would now take emphasis away from the gang symbol. As the tattoo ink machine buzzed away, I thought about what I would tell people when they asked what DEATH BEFORE DISHONOR meant. I would tell them it meant I was ready to die. That if my bros and I were in a jam or shit looked grim, fuck it, I'm ready to die. I would say it meant I was ready to die for the honor of my country. My mind slowly drifted off to visions of a funeral at Arlington, a twenty-one-gun salute, and a crisply folded flag being given to my crying mother.

The tattoo artist snapped me back to reality. "Okay," he said. "We're all done. Take a look." He handed me a mirror. I scanned my new tattoo and then tilted the mirror back down at my gang tattoo. The new message now hovered over the old one.

"Perfect," I said. "That's exactly what I wanted."

Back at base, we began packing for Iraq. My father came to California to take my Camaro back to New Mexico. He gave me some religious articles, including a rosary, a small bottle of holy water, and a Bible that he said my mother wanted me to take to Iraq. I packed them all away for later use.

As Marines packed their bags, we ducked in and out of one another's rooms. An unofficial platoon gathering of salt dogs and boots took place in Egleston's room. There, we made a pact to never surrender. We each agreed that if we ever found ourselves alone and about to be taken prisoner, we would take the enemy down with us instead of being captured alive. Egleston said that in such a situation, he would blow himself up and every terrorist around him with a grenade. We were brothers, all willing to die for one another, we said. And we meant it.

Echo and Fox Companies were scheduled to head off a few days before us. This gave us the chance to witness what it's like to send a Marine off to war. Watching parents and wives and little sons and daughters cling to their daddies . . . well, I don't care how hard you think you are, that scene will damn near rip your heart out. I lit up a Black and Mild cigar and witnessed the whole thing unfold. As I sat there, a wave of rage rolled over me. All this sorrow, all these families, all these little innocent children were having their lives ripped in two because of some cave-dwelling terrorist and a maniacal tyrant that we'd been dealing with for over a decade. I couldn't bear to watch the crying and sadness anymore.

When dawn broke on our day of departure, we gathered our gear and took turns loading M-16 magazines by the dozens while a news crew rolled tape. A reporter asked me a few questions while I was loading.

"Are you scared?" he said.

"Why should I be scared?"

"Because you might die."

"I don't give a fuck about dying."

The reporter looked at me funny. He tried again.

"Umm . . . how do you feel about going to war?"

"It's about time."

He stopped asking me questions and went on to my platoon mates, who also apparently didn't give him the answers he was fishing for. I *wanted* to go to Iraq. Most of us did. Hell, we were grunts. This is what we joined the Corps for—to serve and see combat.

Night fell and families by the dozens drew near. To avoid the media, we would leave at night. All day long, Marines spent time with their families. My family was back in New Mexico, so I spent my time eating and obsessively checking and rechecking my gear that had now been staged in a company formation on the basketball courts outside our barracks.

The agonizing scene was now close at hand, only this time it would be my buddies and their loved ones who would experience it. I lit up another Black and Mild and bullshitted with Magana. I was ready to go. When the time came, the weeping and sniffling and crying grew louder. Moms, sisters, aunts, grandmothers, girlfriends, fiancées, and wives clung to their Marines like Velcro. I distracted myself by checking my gear again. Gunny Linton then yelled the way only a drill instructor can.

"Formation five minutes!"

The wailing grew louder. We really needed to get out of there; the sobbing and the children . . . we needed to leave.

I took another drag off my smoke. *This is your calling,* I remember thinking. *This is what God spared you for.*

Right on time, Gunny called out: "Form for war!"

I let my smoke fall to the ground and snuffed it out with the sole of my boot. It took a few extra minutes to pry all the babies and women away so that Marines could get into formation.

"Attention! Right face!"

Gunny Linton then made the call.

"Off to war!"

The sound of thumping boots smacking the ground in unison echoed through the area.

STOMP, STOMP, STOMP.

I felt the pride I imagine all men before us felt marching with a full combat load off to war. But I'd be lying if I didn't tell you the other emotion I felt. Inside, I felt I was marching to my death. Everything I'd been and done had been so contemptible, so drenched in sin. I couldn't help but feel that God had spared me from my shithead ways only to then fling me onto a battlefield where I would fight and die. If that happened, I was at peace. But inside my soul, I felt my penance was about to be paid in full. And that the price would be my life.

We marched to the battalion parade deck. We loaded onto buses as families watched and wept. After we rode to March Air Force Base, we waited for hours—it seemed like months—for our flight to arrive. When I finally took my seat on the plane to Kuwait, I buckled my seat belt, turned to face the window, and looked out into the darkness.

7

Three Days in a War

lying into Kuwait in late January 2003, the Omni Air commercial airplane we'd been inside for twenty hours must have looked like an untied balloon whizzing and snaking and looping through the air. The erratic flight pattern was intentional. When you fly a commercial plane full of Marines into a war zone, pilots are instructed to use a random route to confuse the enemy and ensure security.

I was surrounded by 200 other Marines of Golf Company, 2nd Battalion, 5th Marine regiment (Golf 2/5), all of us ready for war. Seated to my right was my polar opposite, a Marine named—and I'm not making shit up—Jebediah Mosser, a machine gunner from Louisiana.

The first time I met Jebediah, I remember thinking to myself, *Who the hell names their kid Jebediah?* It sounded like a name from the Bible, except that it's not in the Bible (I looked it up). He was a cool kid, though. I liked the guy.

On the other side of Jebediah sat Jolly, whose bride had the great misfortune of having the first name Molly, therefore making her Molly Jolly. Jolly was good people. He and I had never discussed religion too much, but on the first night of war in Iraq, just before our boots left our AAV (amphibious assault vehicle), he had us all hold hands and bow our heads as he led us in the Lord's Prayer.

That's one of the things you have to love about the U.S. military: They pluck guys from places you didn't even know existed and then toss us all into the great military blender. Where else can a West Coast Mexican and a Louisiana white boy meet and become friends? Where else can you meet a guy whose wife is named Molly Jolly?

Today, in college, my professors blab endlessly about "embracing diversity." They don't know shit about diversity. When your survival depends on the guy next to you, and his depends on you, it's not "diversity" you're embracing—it's your life. It makes no difference whether he's from Utah or Uruguay. In the Corps, it doesn't matter; he's your brother, no matter what. Diversity is hardwired into the Corps. Now we were about to prove that we would put our lives on the line for our brothers.

We were all decked out in second-generation desert cammies, a newer breed of uniform than the "chocolate chip" cammies worn in the Gulf War. Tucked under seats and in overhead compartments were the green Kevlar flak jackets we'd been issued, a brilliant color choice that ensured we'd look like a line of marching olives, each one ripe for enemy shooting against the sandy desert background. We wanted to know who the genius was who decided not to make desert gear a regularly issued set of gear. No money in the budget, I guess.

As Marines, we'd gotten used to always getting the shittiest equipment. Truth be told, in a weird way, we took pride in it. Army always gets better equipment. So our attitude is "Fuck it. Give Army the good stuff. We'll take the scraps."

The plane's wheels kissed ground around midnight Kuwaiti

time. All I could think about was grabbing my rifle from the cargo cases stored in the belly of the plane. When the cabin door flung open it felt like a hair dryer blasting in my face. The temperature was 90 degrees, but it's the humidity that takes your breath away.

Descending the steps onto the tarmac, each of us was given our rifle. The number of tents and vehicles and military personnel present made it feel like the entire Armed Forces had been assembled. Rifle in hand, we all stood in the early-morning air and took in our new surroundings.

"Gas! Gas! Gas!" someone yelled.

I scrambled for my gas mask.

Shit. Shit. Shit.

We were all scraping and clawing at our gear. We must have looked like a bunch of fucking rookie idiots. *Some liberators,* the Kuwaitis must have been thinking. *No sooner do these Americans get off the plane than they trigger Saddam to launch an NBC (nuclear, biological, chemical) attack on our people.* But if we looked funny, you should have seen some of the Kuwaitis—they were freaking out. There we all were, only three minutes in-country, sweating like pigs, surrounded by Kuwaitis who were yelling and flailing their arms while seeking cover.

"Time!" yelled Captain Hammond. "You guys would have already been dead. You're lucky that was just a drill. This is no joke, gents. You will tighten up! Remember, you are now in a 360-degree threat zone. Wake up!" Captain Hammond was a great commanding officer (CO). He was a lighter-skinned African American and very intellectual. He knew how to get the most mileage out of his Marines. The gas drill on the tarmac was to be the first of endless drills and lessons we would receive during the weeks leading up to the invasion.

After receiving two magazines, each with thirty rounds, we piled into a bunch of civilian buses.

"Shut the curtains!" someone yelled.

The sound of sliding curtains zipped through the bus. Now in darkness, we wondered why the hell we had to sit for hours inside stationary, drape-drawn buses wearing our full gear. Furthermore, I kept thinking, *Why aren't we being transported by U.S. military vehicles and personnel?* But it was the driver more than anything that had me a little concerned. Lieutenant Maurer, also known as "Gator" or "Mau Mau," got on the bus and instructed Tardif and me to load our rifles and maintain security. As soon as the driver saw us load our rifles, he got visibly nervous and started acting shady. Tardif glanced at me. I glanced at Tardif. And the look on both our faces said, *What the fuck is up with this guy?*

The buses fired up and we began the drive to living support area 5 (LSA-5). Lieutenant Maurer explained that a few convoys had already taken small-arms fire in transit, so I sat on the bus steps and eyeballed the passing cars. Mercedes-Benz must make a killing in Kuwait, because it seemed like every car that passed was one. The landscape, however, looked like a wasteland. Just rolling sand dunes as far as the eye could see. After a tense hour of driving, we made it to LSA-5. It was little more than a few large white command post (CP)–style tents that had been provided by the Kuwaiti government. It was now early afternoon local time, and the temperature was a blazing 120 degrees.

We set up our two-man tents in organized rows and columns. Garcia and I were hooch mates. The following day, it was announced that Golf Company would be hiking to see some general deliver a speech. Everybody was pissed that we had to hike to get a "moto speech" (motivational speech). I began packing my gear for the hike when Staff Sergeant Sikes, a super-smart Midwesterner and stellar staff sergeant of my platoon, approached and told me I was going to pull security for the camp while the company was gone. I perked up, grabbed my desert camouflage bandanna, tied it around my neck gangster style, and made my way to the fighting hole from which another Marine and I would pull security. I slammed a rifle magazine in the magazine well, but per my orders, I kept my weapon in condition three (magazine inserted but with no round locked in the chamber). Sand was blowing everywhere, so I pulled my cammo rag up over my nose and face like I was about to put in work for my old gang, which made me laugh a little.

A short time later, reporter Mike Cerre, who was embedded with Fox 2/5, walked up with a cameraman.

"Hey, Marine," he said. "Your living standards have just gone way down. How do you feel about that?"

"We're used to living like dogs," I replied. "This is just the same shit, different place."

"The weather is hot and the sand is brutal. Do you think you're ready to go to war?"

"This ain't shit. I've been through worse shit than this. I'm ready for war. Send me north."

For the most part, the reporters I came into contact with were fairly decent, at least to your face. But we weren't suckers. We knew damn well what many of them were up to. They'd be all buddy-buddy, only to later shaft you and your brothers by filing bullshit stories about how we got "bogged down" just days into the invasion. Or they'd find the one shitbag in the U.S. military—the sour little bitch of Operation Iraqi Freedom—who hated on the Corps or was pissed because Mommy wasn't there to wipe his ass and then turn him into the poster boy and official spokesman of the military.

Contrary to what John Kerry would have you believe, we're not that stupid. But whatever. Liberal media just go with the territory, I guess. They had news to spin. We had terrorists to kill.

IN THE DAYS AHEAD, the battalion commander (BC) announced that 5th Marines would be setting up a TAA (Tactical Assembly Area) three miles away. This would be our new home. So each of us lugged over 200 pounds of gear the three miles. To put on our packs, we had to lay the packs on the ground, straps up, and then lie on the packs before having someone pull us up to counterbalance the weight. I felt especially bad for the guys in weapons platoon tasked with carrying our crew-served weapons. Everybody saddled up and we stepped off in our two tight columns and began the trek.

The weak hikers felt the pain almost immediately. Many people fell back. We hadn't gone that far and already we had to take a break. When we stepped off again, our two columns were loose and ragged, like nomads wandering through the desert. The goal now was simply to get there. The upper-left side of the plastic frame on my MOLLE pack snapped, sending all the pack's weight to my right, which caused me to stutter-step a little. My right arm fell asleep. My fingers felt like sausages and the needles were starting to hurt. As a fire team leader, however, you learn that everything you do—verbally or nonverbally—gives your team license or incentive to do as you do. I tried to hide my now purple-and-red hand and to keep up with the hike.

When we arrived at our destination, we broke up into platoons with attachments and set up in defense. Any guy who's been to Kuwait will tell you that digging your fighting hole can sometimes take hours. It's like digging in a beach made of sugar; the fine-grained sand caves in on your hole. By nightfall, most of us had decent holes.

Nighttime in the Kuwaiti Desert can send a shiver up your spine. The temperature can plummet. On 2:00 A.M. fire watch, I had to wear my gloves, watch cap, and green USMC sweatshirt under my uniform. Through my frosty breath I scanned the terrain with my night-vision goggles (NVGs) and occasionally looked up at the stars in all their beautiful serenity.

But the novelty of our new surroundings quickly wore off. I'd always heard and read combat vets say that war is 10 percent action and 90 percent waiting. Depending on your MOS, that's not too far from the truth. But basically life started to feel like that movie *Groundhog Day* with Bill Murray, in which the same monotonous shit happens every single day. Stand two at reveille. Chow on an MRE. Clean weapons. Gas drill. Work on your fighting holes. Gas drill. Clean weapons. Chow on an MRE. Work on your fighting holes. Chow on an MRE. Gas drill. Clean weapons. Train. Sleep. Fire watch. Then stand two at reveille and do it all over again.

The only real change to our routine was that on some nights and mornings we'd get food trucked out to us that had been prepared by the cooks. I say "food." It was almost comical how bad it was. It was some *Oliver Twist* gruel. It wasn't the cooks' fault. We were in the middle of a desert waiting for a war to erupt. Shit, at least they tried to feed us.

A week into living at the TAA, the tents we'd been issued started falling apart. They had been made for civilian use, not made for the abuse grunts would inflict. I wasn't complaining. To tell you the truth, I was surprised when we *got* tents. The Marine Corps could have easily said, "Fuck you. No tents." No, I guess the only real thing about the living conditions that sucked was that (a) the water we had to drink tasted like bleach and (b) the smallpox shot we'd all received back in the States had yet to heal and wouldn't stop oozing fluid.

Weeks later, it was announced that we would patrol back to LSA-5 for a few days to rest. It sounded good to me. Rumor had it that in the few short weeks we were in the TAA, LSA-5 had been transformed into a tent city with showers, something none of us had seen in almost four weeks now. The rumor proved to be true. Some of us opted to wait until later that night so that the lines would die down. Bad move. By the time my turn rolled around and I yanked back the shower curtain, a clogged drain and a foul, brown cesspool greeted me. *Fuck it,* I thought. I sunk my feet down into the ankle-deep sludge and scrubbed down in record time. It felt damn good to be clean again.

Another enjoyable experience was the moto speech that our commander, General Matis, delivered a few days later. We were happy to see him. Unlike a lot of other generals, he could deliver a helluva motivational speech. I always liked when he would call us his "fine young men." General Matis had a Marine sense of humor and struck me as a great leader. Every time I saw or heard him, I just envisioned him as being that kind of commander who would be in the front of a charge on a white horse, wielding a hefty sword—who would say something inspirational, make his horse rear up on its hind legs, point his sword toward the enemy, and charge into battle.

Yet no moto speech could have prepared me for the way I'd feel two days later when we went to the intelligence tent for a short briefing on the current situation in Iraq. Inside the tent, we were shown the surveillance and satellite photos. They were thick with masses of Saddam's forces who were assembling in the narrow, building-lined streets of Baghdad. A wave of inevitable doom washed over me. Taking in the intelligence images made me reflect back on all the stupid, thuggish bullshit I'd previously been involved in. All of those old images seemed so silly, so comical—like watching goofy home movies of your first T-ball game or your first steps. Looking at those city streets in black-and-white photographs was when the gravity of it all set in. I was going to war.

We left the tent in a daze, but carried on with our normal routine. That night, we all perked up when it was announced that there would be a steak dinner—a rare treat at a time when we were already rationing our MREs. Second helpings on steaks weren't allowed, so Tardif and I put our infantry skills to good use to address the hunger problem. He stood guard while I snuck inside the cooks' food-prep tent and snagged as many bread rolls as I could carry. We then switched up and he loaded up with rolls as I stood guard. It was quite a haul for our platoon.

Following our bread heist, I went to visit a friend of mine who worked in supply. When I entered his tent, I noticed that only a dozen or so Marines lived there, compared to the 125 or so guys crammed into each of Golf Company's two tents.

"Must be nice!" I yelled.

My buddy Gutierrez, nicknamed "Indio," turned around.

"What's up, dawg?"

"Shit, man, I'm trying to live like you," I said.

I pointed to the juice boxes, fresh fruit, and ample space inside the tent.

"You should have been a POG!" he said.

I laughed. "No shit!"

"Fucking grunts," he said with a laugh when he saw me suck down an apple juice.

That's what we were—fucking grunts, different from the others. Infantrymen's preparations for battle, and even our modes of transportation, were unique. When we weren't traveling by foot, our amphibious assault vehicles (AAV, "amtrac," or just "trac") were our primary mode of transport. An AAV is sort of like a big metal box on tracks. If you really jam Marines in tight, you can squeeze about twenty-two guys into one. The seat inside a trac is no bigger than your average school lunch bench. So with all your gear on, you're lucky if half your ass stays on the seat. We lucked out and got cool trackers. And that's important, because your trackers are part transportation service, part gunners. Our trac, 202, was run by Sergeant Smith, who hailed from Houston, Texas, and was on "stop loss" (when the military freezes, and temporarily extends, your contract). To prepare for combat, the USMC made sure we spent ample time practicing lightning rear dismounts.

Later that week, we were told we'd be going on a trac movement. However, they conveniently left off how long it would last. If I'd known at the time, I'd have probably hidden in my fighting hole. All of 2nd Squad and attachments, twenty guys in all, packed into our trac. Along with me were Tardif, Garcia, Birdsong, Miguel, De La Feunte, Siler, Welsand, Terrone, Elias, Cortez, Cherrilo, Staff Sergeant Pettigrew, Doc Chili, Jolly, Hot Rod, Hash, Wallender, Smith, and Donnelly. To create a realistic simulation, we were made to travel with the gear on that we would carry during any eventual invasion of Iraq. For this practice run, we would be moving buttoned up, which meant the two huge doors on top of the trac would remain closed. We'd be "sealed" inside the dark vault.

Despite our being packed in like sardines, hour one passed without a hitch. Hour two, no sweat. Hour three, I was still good. Hot, but good. Hour four and now shit was starting to get uncomfortable. Thankfully, the ramps dropped and we rushed out and got into a hasty defense. Night had now fallen and I had no clue where we were (as if it would have made a difference even if I did; everything looked the same—rolling sandy dunes and chilly winds whipping through the air). Fifteen minutes later, we loaded back into the tracs. Hour five and your ass felt like you were sitting on thumbtacks due to the hard steel bench. When hour six rolled around, the vehicle's erratic movements combined with the hilly terrain threw us bumping into one another. Moans and groans could now be heard inside the trac. I happened to be seated next to Elias, an oversized El Salvadoran guy known for chronic bitching during situations we could not change. He wouldn't shut up (he was a cool guy otherwise). The claustrophobic quarters combined with Elias's bitching welled up the strange and intense desire to scream out loud like a psycho. But I resisted the temptation.

Hour seven and now guys were openly yelling at one another and wanting to throw down because of the way somebody was sitting. This shit was getting beyond any level of discomfort most of us had ever felt. Hour eight and we started asking one another what the fuck we were doing and just what kind of "trac movement" this was. At hour nine, all the body heat had turned our metal box on tracks into an oven. Hour ten, and now people were engaged in small fist-fights, which was a feat in and of itself because you could barely move around to begin with.

The eleventh damn hour—almost half the motherfucking day—dropped and I'd had it with the massive bench hog beside me. In fairness, Elias wasn't trying to squish my 160-pound frame—he was just a damn beast.

"Elias, if you don't move over, I'm going to stab you," I said.

"Fuck you," he said. "I'll stab you back."

We snapped out of it and apologized to each other. Everyone was starting to lose it. Hours thirteen, fourteen, and fifteen came and went and all conversation ceased; we'd been beaten into submission. There was no choice but to take it. *Finally,* the ramps dropped and we were back at the TAA. We staggered out of the trac like a bunch of drunken hobos with a fresh perspective on the true definition of the word "discomfort." And that, of course, had been precisely the point. They were preparing us for the way our lives would be for the next three months.

A FEW DAYS LATER, we patrolled back to the LSA. Once there, I made an effort to catch up with friends I hadn't had a chance to talk to much since we left Oki. I ran into Padilla, a buddy of mine from Norwalk, California. Padilla offered me a Black and Mild, my favorite ghetto cigar, and we talked about what lay ahead.

"So you ready for this war?" he asked.

"I just really don't give a fuck," I said. "I'm as ready as I'll ever be."

"Me, too."

"How was your trac ride?"

"Don't even ask. Shit, man."

When I returned to my platoon, Magana and I discussed what we were going to do with our money when and if we got back to the States. We both agreed that we'd buy Rolexes. It became a running joke between us. Anytime shit got bad in Iraq, we'd just shake our wrists at each other and laugh. "Just keep that Rolex in mind, dawg."

By this point, rumors were circulating that we might not be going to war in Iraq after all. Some stories said that Saddam had already given in to President Bush's demands, while others said that this had all just been a show of force, symbolic muscle flexing. The rumor mill got so out of control that Magana decided to take people's minds off the "no war" stories by creating some new, more-interesting rumors. I watched him walk over to 2nd Platoon's side of the tent and work his plan.

"Hey, did you hear the news?" he said. "J-Lo [Jennifer Lopez] died!"

"What?" a gullible Marine replied. "She died?"

"Yeah," he said. "She died in a car crash!"

The J-Lo rumor spread like cancer through all of LSA-5. It was amazing how viral that shit was. Everyone was talking about J-Lo's "tragic death" and all about her "fatal car crash." With no Internet nearby, no one had any real way to confirm it. We were disconnected from all means of communication. We couldn't discern between fact and fiction.

THE NEXT MORNING, Staff Sergeant Sikes selected me to go to Camp Commando with him and some others. Everyone in the platoon gave me money to buy things at the PX. But the main reason for the trip was so that Marines who had wives stationed in Kuwait could see them. So we rode from camp to camp dropping guys off to see their wives before we ended up at Camp Commando. Once that was complete, I headed to a nearby chow hall with Rodriguez-Garcia, better known as Rod-Gar, or just RG. When we moved up in the chow line and into the tent, I was astonished. It was a full chow hall with a massive buffet. Drinks, ice cream . . . you name it. Here we were living like jackals and these people were living like kings. I piled as much as I could on my tray. On the way to get some orange juice from the refrigerator, I bumped into a pretty Latina Marine. These bastards had everything!

Rod-Gar and I sat down at our table, and the second before I took the first forkful of food, the gas siren sounded. We both quickly donned and cleared our gas masks and sat motionless, staring through the lenses of our gas masks. *Motherfucker!* I thought. Rod-Gar just shook his head in disappointment. I sat lusting after the food, imagining how good it probably tasted. Fifteen minutes later, the all-clear sign came through. We ripped off our masks and ate like wolves. For over a month, all we'd eaten were MREs and *Oliver Twist* slop.

When we went back to get some more food, we noticed that we were drawing a few stares from other troops. While we were eating, a few soldiers and some Marines approached us.

"What are those devices on your rifles?" they asked.

"What are you talking about?" I said.

They pointed to our Pac-4s, which are infrared laser devices that produce a beam that can only be seen with night-vision goggles.

"Oh, that? That's a Pac-4," I said.

Rod-Gar was busy inhaling an ice cream, so I explained to them about the lasers. Then I noticed that I was the only person with an M-203 grenade launcher attached to his rifle.

"Are you guys Recon?" they asked.

"Naw, man. We're just regular grunts."

"Can I see your rifle and check out the Pac-4?" one said.

"Fuck no! This is *my* rifle," I said like a jealous boyfriend. "And nobody touches her except me."

With that they left, allowing Rod-Gar and me to achieve our goal of eating ice cream bars until we got sick. When we got back to the TAA, I divvied up all the candy and cigarettes (two-carton maximum) I'd bought according to how much each person had given me. It was kind of funny to see the whole company eating candy like school kids. But this was a luxury, and we were going to enjoy it.

Later that night, I grabbed my helmet and a pen. I decided I wanted to ink it up, just like generations of combat Marines had done before us. "Kevlar art" tells a lot about an individual—where his head is. I didn't want to write some cheesy slogan, so I settled on a word: "POISON." In my best "tagger-style" Old English script, I blazed the word across the back of my Kevlar cover. As I inked the cloth, several Marines looked on to see what I was writing. I got several compliments on how nice my handwriting looked (if only they knew!). I figured I wouldn't catch any bullshit, because the word wasn't vulgar or politically incorrect.

Well, I figured wrong. A few days later, as I was getting out of my fighting hole to wash out my canteen cup, Staff Sergeant Sikes yelled, "Martinez! Get over here right now!"

I ran over to him, wondering what I'd done wrong.

"What the *hell* is that on your Kevlar cover?"

"It says 'POISON,' Staff Sergeant."

"Why the *hell* did you write 'poison' on your Kevlar?"

I then said jokingly, "Because if you fuck with poison, it will fuck you up."

The staff sergeant didn't think I was funny.

"Who gave you permission to write on your Kevlar?" he demanded.

"Nobody, Staff Sergeant."

"No one is allowed to write *anything* on their Kevlars."

"But Staff Sergeant, it doesn't say anything offensive," I protested.

"Doesn't matter. Nobody is allowed to write shit on their Kevlar per BC [battalion commander] orders."

"But Staff Sergeant . . ."

"But nothing. Take that shit off right now and show me when you do," he said.

I scuffed back to my hole cursing and covered the helmet art with a piece of camouflage tape. As I was taping my Kevlar, I heard the staff sergeant rip into Dreyer for writing on his helmet. Garcia and Tardif agreed with me, but there was no use in arguing. Not even symbols would be allowed. When some Marines drew the Ace of Spades on their Kevlars as a tribute to the Vietnam-era Marines, they were made to cover them up, too. So much for freedom of expression.

After nightfall, I did another thing I'd wanted to do. At 0130, I got up and walked outside the tent with my MOLLE pack. After rummaging through, I found the religious items my mother had asked my father to give me before I headed off to Iraq. I laid out all my gear around my fighting hole. And then I prayed. I asked God to be with me in battle. I asked that He watch over me and give me the strength to survive. As I prayed, I sprinkled holy water on myself, my load-bearing vest, flak jacket, SAPI plates, MOLLE pack, Kevlar, rifle magazines, NVGs, the sights of my M-203, front and rear sights of my M-16, and the triggers of both weapons. If I was to meet the sword of death, I asked that He make it quick and precise. I then asked God to help me do the right thing if I was ever confused during battle. I prayed that my rounds be well-aimed and that they pierce the hearts of my enemies. I ended my prayer with the Rifleman's Creed, a final act of unity between me and my weapon.

The next several days were spent at LSA-5 preparing for what now seemed inevitable—war. But not before we received critical news. Following a battalion PT session, the battalion commander (BC) issued an important announcement: Jennifer Lopez was, in fact, very much alive. I glanced over at Magana, who was trying to contain his laughter. But with the safety and security of the beloved Puerto Rican booty now assured, we could all rest easy.

That afternoon and evening, I did what had become my routine. I endlessly checked, rechecked, and rearranged my ALICE (All-Purpose Lightweight Individual Carrying Equipment) gear in different configurations to determine which one was most tactically sound. That night, the sound of blades dragging across sharpening blocks sliced through the tent. All of us sat focused and deep in thought while sharpening our KA-BARs before going to sleep. Hours later, the tent lights flicked on. Guys woke up cursing at no one in particular. When my eyes adjusted to the light, I thought I was dreaming. Staff Sergeant Sikes was standing before us bathed in light.

"We have gotten the order for war," he said. "Gather your things. There is a company formation outside in ten minutes." I shot up and started packing my things.

Within minutes, most of us were outside and waiting in loose formation. Captain Hammond spoke: "President Bush has given Saddam and his two sons an ultimatum. He ordered Saddam and his sons to either get out of Iraq within forty-eight hours or be prepared to face decisive military action. Gentlemen, that was forty-eight hours ago. Saddam and his sons, Uday and Kusay, have refused to leave. That was their first mistake. Their second mistake was not factoring in the Marines massed near their border. We will now travel to our DA [dispersal area], which is called 'Bear.' This will be our jump-off point into the invasion. After this, gents, there is no turning back—we will be crossing the LOD [Line of Departure]."

The entire company erupted into cheers. Within minutes, the tracs pulled up for loading. As we rode north, no one spoke. Adrenaline surged. A few hours later, when we got to our DA and the ramps dropped, the sun was breaking the horizon. We set up in a long defensive line facing north toward Iraq. Iraq, we were told, was now only five miles away. We cloaked our AAVs in cammie netting to camouflage their positions. We were told only to dig skirmisher trenches. We wouldn't be there long.

Later that day, we held a "grunt Christmas." Palette after palette of ammo and explosives were put before us for the taking. The one rule was to take only as much as you could reasonably carry. I filled my 40 mm vest with 203 rounds and took 26 High Explosive Dual

Purpose (HEDP) rounds. Then I equipped myself with a red star and a white star cluster, two illumination rounds, six grenades, and an ammo can of 5.56. I filled each of my fourteen magazines with 5.56 rounds. We next helped our SMAW (shoulder-launched multi-purpose assault weapon) and machine-gun attachments load up before weighing down the trac with rockets, C-4 detonation cord, and a variety of other explosives that the 0351s would use. We packed the trac with ammo can after ammo can of linked 7.62 rounds for the M-240 Golf, and we made sure to take several AT-4 rockets, which we stashed inside the trac.

After arming ourselves, we wrote "death notes" to our loved ones. This is what I remember writing to my mother:

Mom,

If you are reading this, I'm dead. Don't be mad because I'm not mad. I'm sorry for all the grief I caused you in my middle school and high school years. I love you very much. Please bury me in the Arlington or Albuquerque military cemeteries. I'll see you in heaven.

—Marco

I turned in my letter and tried to forget about dying. The BC, the sergeant major, and the battalion chaplain held a company formation. The BC gave a moto speech. The thing I remember most is when he said, "We will now exact our revenge on a regime that has not let a people live in peace for decades." The sergeant major was up next. He, too, gave a moto speech, saying, "You now have the world looking at you. When you cross the LOD, let's show the terrorists why the world's tyrants fear the Marines!" The chaplain was the anchorman. He gave a prayer and blessed us. He then told us a story from the Bible about warfare. I wish I could remember the story or where it's found in the Bible. But it felt right in my soul. It fit.

That night, we slept in our skimpy ranger rolls, which were little more than a poncho and a poncho liner tied together to create a weather-resistant blanket. This allowed us to move at a moment's notice. When the sun came up, we cleaned weapons. By noon, we were told that since we were so close to the Iraqi border, we had to go to the bathroom in pairs. I had to take a shit, so I grabbed one of my boots, Terrone. Not surprisingly, when I found him, he was singing a Frank Sinatra medley.

"Where we going, Corporal?" he asked.

"You're going to serenade me while I take a shit," I said.

"Umm . . . okay."

We went to an area away from the company. I brought my E-tool so that I could sit instead of squat. An E-tool is a miniature shovel whose head folds down to be more compact. I put my E-tool in an L shape and handed my rifle to Terrone.

"Keep an eye out for Iraqi soldiers," I said.

"Roger that."

I sat on the head of the E-tool with one ass cheek on it and one off.

"Well, Terrone, serenade me!"

"What song do you want me to sing, Corporal?"

"I don't care, just sing!"

Terrone launched into some classic Sinatra. I have to hand it to the guy, he could actually carry a tune.

"Nice!" I said.

I quickly finished and we headed back to the company.

"I can't believe that just happened," he said.

"What? I don't rate a serenade?"

When we got back, the company had passed the news that 1st

Force Reconnaissance was going to take down Safwan Hill, which was the highest point in southern Iraq. The Iraqi Army had an observation post on the hill and 1st Force was going to knock it the fuck out. That night, under the cover of darkness, 1st Force infiltrated the border undetected and strategically took out enemy personnel and everything else in sight. We expected to spend another night cold to the bone. Instead, the United States bombed Baghdad. We were now one day into a war.

We could see Navy ships launching Tomahawk cruise missiles. Iraqi Scud missiles filled the sky like fireflies. Gauging from their trajectory, many of the Scuds were headed for Kuwait City and American bases like Doha. Some were headed for us and landed not far from our position. But Patriot missiles knocked down just about every Scud in the sky. It sounded like cars colliding, only in midair.

We tore off the cammie netting that covered each trac, loaded in, and closed the ramps. A count was taken to ensure that each trac had all its men.

"Grab hands and bow your heads," a voice said. It was Jolly. "Our Father, who art in heaven, hallowed be thy name . . ."

After the Lord's Prayer, we rolled out. We were buttoned up with no air watch or lights (we were moving full tactical). Sitting inside our darkened AAV, I turned toward Tardif, our squad leader.

"Are you ready for this?" I asked.

"Hell yes," he said.

Tardif then yelled, "2nd Squad, are you ready to get some?"

The trac echoed with "Ooh-rahs," "Kills," and "Errs" (a Marine's way of expressing enthusiasm).

We listened to the radio net that broadcast the entire company's radio transmissions. Kuwaitis and U.S. military combat engineers planned to breach several areas along the Kuwaiti defense line. According to the radio, we were now one mile from the Iraq border.

"Lock and load!" Tardif yelled.

A volley of bolts being pulled to the rear by their charging handle clicked through the trac, followed by the loud snap of the buffer spring pushing the bolt forward to chamber a round. After some stop and go, our trackers informed us we were at the breach sight. Within five minutes, however, our trac hit a tank trap that was part of the Kuwaiti border defense. Our trac nose-dived, slamming us to the front of the vehicle. The jumble of bodies was then thrown to the rear as our trac climbed the incline out from the tank trap. We sustained only some minor bruises in the process, but traversing the trap was significant nonetheless. We were now officially inside Iraq.

Our trac took its place in the tactical formation that had gathered on the Iraq side. A mechanized battle was taking place some distance ahead of us, 500 meters or so. Round after round of tank fire was all we could hear. We were instructed to "unbutton." So we opened the two big heavy doors on the top of the trac and pulled air watch. As soon as we flung open the doors, the smell of smoke smacked you in the nose. Siler and Birdsong took air watch. I joined Birdsong (the SAW gunner for my fire team), a blond-haired kid from Arkansas, on the right side of the trac. It was completely dark. You couldn't see anything, so I pulled down my NVGs from my Kevlar and scanned the area. Off in the distance, tanks burned. I couldn't make out whether they were ours or the enemy's.

Under the powerful protection of our M1-A1 Abrams tanks, we pushed forward toward our first objective, securing the Rumaylah oil fields. Penetrating farther into Iraq, we began to see just how devastating U.S. tanks and air strikes had been. Scorched corpses and charred torsos with missing legs and heads were strewn across our path as we trekked north. Even as I write these words, I can still see those blackened human frames, seemingly frozen in time. They looked petrified, as in the wood, not the emotion, although I'm sure they had been that, too.

The sight made me . . . *envious.* These now-charred and crispy enemy soldiers weren't our kills. They belonged to someone else. These guys had spent all night trying to kill us and our brother Marines. But we didn't "get some." Someone else got some. I wanted action. I wanted to get mine.

On the first sunrise of the invasion—the very next day—we arrived at the Rumaylah oil fields. The smell of chemicals and burning oil made some Marines cough.

"Hey, look on the bright side," someone said. "At least now we've solved the mystery of what caused Gulf War Syndrome!"

The ramps dropped. Intel reports indicated that enemy forces of battalion strength were in the area. But we didn't see anyone. Across the flat, craggy terrain, all we could make out were oil-processing facilities that looked like a tangle of metal pipes and clusters of oil worker apartments built by an architect with no imagination. Staff Sergeant Sikes informed us to clear the area. Captain Hammond and the rest of the officers spent fifteen minutes devising a defensive plan in the event we came into contact with the enemy. Squads of twenty Marines would split up and begin patrolling the area.

Because Egleston was the senior corporal over Tardif, he led the patrol. He directed us to move forward with our weapons at the ready. We had no tank support and were out of the sight and safety of the .50 caliber machine guns on our AAVs. We walked into the wall of 120-degree heat on high alert, ready for an ambush. And that's when we heard enemy firing shots one hundred meters away.

Pop. Pop. Pop.

We all rotated in the direction of the sound and there, in the distance, stood a gang of approximately 150 Iraqi soldiers. Spying them through binoculars, a teammate said they were locked and loaded, some of them carrying RPG (rocket-propelled grenade) launchers and AK-47s. Twenty U.S. Marines versus 150 Iraqis were shitty odds. But this is what we'd come to do. The adrenaline was surging.

Out from the center of the gang of Iraqis, a figure stepped forward and started walking toward us.

"What the fuck is he doing?" a few of us yelled. "Light him up!"

"No!" Egleston yelled. "Just hold on."

The man walked halfway between us and his men. There, in the middle of the firing lane, stood an Iraqi colonel, decked out in full uniform. The guy could have been Saddam's twin brother. He even had the thick black mustache. All twenty of our rifles were pointed at him. But the Iraqi colonel stepped closer and began yelling something in Arabic while waving a white T-shirt. Egleston whipped out the two-page pamphlet we'd been given to help us interpret and speak different Arabic phrases.

"No shoot! No shoot!" yelled the Iraqi leader in English. "No shoot! No shoot!"

"Hold your fire," Egleston said. Egleston then yelled in Arabic for the Iraqi colonel to "Lie down! Lie down!"

We had been warned that the Iraqis might not fight fair. This could be a setup. With 150 of his men standing in the distance, the last thing we needed was to walk out into the firing lane only to get lit up by his men. Through my iron sights, I watched the enemy leader drop to his knees, sit on his feet, and put his hands behind his back. Egleston and Bodine searched and zipcuffed him. The only weapon they found on him was a flashy 9 mm pistol that looked like one of those fancy collector models, only his had elegant Arabic scrawlings all over the pistol. Later, when Bodine showed the pistol to an interpreter, he told us the scrawlings read "Death to the West." There was a single round inside the chamber.

Miguel and I took the colonel to the "pig pen," an area we'd taped off to serve as a place to process prisoners of war. Miguel, a 5'8" Mexican American and former soccer player, was the right guy for the job. His status as a former Christian missionary to South America made him the compassionate, humanitarian type. That said, when the time came to lock and load, he was one of the most intense killers on the battlefield. A God-fearing grunt, but a grunt nonetheless.

The Iraqi colonel looked at my brown skin.

"Kuwaiti?" he asked.

"No, no. American!" I said.

"Kuwaiti?" he said nervously.

"No! American! Shut the fuck up!"

Miguel and I then turned him over to an officer for interrogation before returning to our squad.

"The rest of them are coming!" someone said.

The mob of armed Iraqis was now walking toward us. They'd just seen their leader taken. We were on heightened alert and ready if they wanted a fight. I raised my rifle into shooting position. Half wore uniforms, and the other half were in civilian rags. Some were holding AK-47s at the alert position. They were now fifty meters away and getting closer.

"Do something, motherfuckers!" I said. "Let's fucking go!"

I had my front sight centered in the rear sight. Peering at the armed swarm, I moved my rifle from man to man. Squinting through our rifle sights, we could see that they looked much older than us. They were in their thirties or forties.

"Do it, motherfuckers! Do it!" another Marine yelled.

They kept coming closer.

"Can we shoot? Can we smoke 'em?" we yelled.

"Hold your fucking fire!" Egleston barked.

And that's when some in the herd grabbed their AK-47 front stock with one hand and the butt stock with the other as they put their rifles overhead to indicate surrender.

"U.S. Marines. Stop! Throw down your weapons!" we yelled.

One by one, the enemy began tossing aside their weapons. Just as their colonel had done, they got down on their knees and raised their hands into the air. They looked thirsty and tired. After searching and zipcuffing them, we walked through the group pouring water from our canteens into their mouths like mother birds feeding worms to hungry hatchlings.

We processed the POWs and began receiving backup support from other units and British Marines. The Brits were cool guys, and we all got along really well. But even with their assistance, we were quickly overwhelmed. More and more groups of enemy soldiers made their way toward us and surrendered. We finally received orders to collect their weapons and then just turn the Iraqis away—a bad decision, I thought.

With the POWs detained and processed, that night we linked back up with the rest of Golf Company and resumed guarding the Rumaylah oil fields. All Golf Company Marines were instructed to get in groups of two and spread out into a massive U-shape, with each pair roughly twenty-five yards apart. I linked up with my hooch mate, Garcia. Once we paired off, we were to dig fighting holes. No sooner had the tips of E-tools penetrated the dirt than we heard what sounded like coins dropping into a tin can.

Tink. Tink. Tink. Tink.

Rocks lay just six inches beneath the dirt surface; digging was futile. So we dropped our packs and used them as concealment instead. After staring at the motionless terrain in front of us for a few hours, I needed to use the bathroom. I grabbed Birdsong, who was in the hole next to mine, to be my shadow. Birdsong spoke with an

Arkansas twang and was country as hell. But what was funny was that the guy was really into hip-hop and often freestyled. The other thing about Birdsong was that the guy might as well have been a theologian; he had serious Bible-quoting skills.

Birdsong and I cautiously made our way to a concealed area so I could piss. We crept over a large berm, only to make a surprising discovery. The Iraqi soldiers who had surrendered had established a defensive line with a couple of large-caliber machine guns that were locked, loaded, oiled, and ready to go. There were also hundreds of mortar rounds with enough mortar tubes to wreak havoc. I looked through the sights of one of the machine guns. They could have hit us and hit us good on our initial approach up to the oil fields.

At approximately 10 P.M., we received news over the radio net: The remnants of the 51st Mechanized Iraqi Infantry Division were spotted traveling toward our position. Much of the 51st had been destroyed near Nasiriyah, but elements remained and were on the move. Captain Hammond immediately radioed for air support. No good. Air was taken up in Nasiriyah and wouldn't be available for some time, we were told. Our Javelin gunners went on high alert. Our only source of light came from the orange glow of the "eternal flames," the oil towers with a flame like a lit match that burned continuously. Garcia and I lay flat on our stomachs, shoulder-to-shoulder, behind our packs.

"Can you fucking believe this shit?" Garcia said. "We've got no air support, no tanks, and now we're about to die up in this bitch like this."

"Well, if we're going to get smoked," I said, "let's at least fuck them up in the process. Hold on a sec. I'll be right back."

I sprung up from the ground and dashed over to our AAV. If we were anxious about the 51st Mechanized Division's arrival, the trackers were wide-eyed. I started rooting around in the back of the

AAV for an AT-4—an antiarmor weapon used for knocking out tanks. With a worried look on his face, Donnelly, the mechanic, stopped me.

"You heard the 51st is coming, right?" he said.

"Yeah, fool, that's why I'm getting an AT-4."

A few hours later, we were told the 51st Mechanized Division was in front of us off in the distance. Garcia and I lay side by side, staring through the puffs of icy breath coming from our mouths. The .50 cal. gunners atop our company's twelve AAVs were in position and gripping the guns. But everyone knew damn well that a company's worth of rifles and twelve .50 cal. guns were nothing compared to the firepower of a mechanized division. Not to mention the fact that our AAVs were the old kind without the thermal sights.

We were, in a word, fucked.

The radios inside our helmets started crackling. A garbled, static-filled voice was trying to say something. But I couldn't make out what that was. I looked at Garcia, who was equally confused. The voice repeated the message again, yet neither of us could decipher it. The voice said the message a third and final time, and at last we understood.

"Open your mouth!" the voice said. "I repeat, open your mouth!"

An F-16 screamed overhead.

BOOM!!!

The night turned into day.

"Oh shit!" Garcia yelled.

Five hundred meters in front of us was the biggest, loudest explosion I'd ever seen or heard in my life. The ground shook under us. The reason you open your mouth is so the pressure from the bomb doesn't explode your eardrums. The roar of a second jet's afterburner screeched.

BOOM!!!

"Yeah, get some, motherfuckers," I said under my breath.

The combined heat of two explosions felt like I had stuck my head inside an oven. During training, you're taught not to look directly at an explosion. But my eyeballs turned into moths; I couldn't take my eyes off the sight. Neither could Garcia. We lay like two jackasses watching the explosions. When I looked away from the white fire, my eyes took a second to adjust.

We later learned that our forward air controller (FAC) had relayed coordinates to our guardian angel, two F-16s that had been freed up from delivering the "Shock and Awe" elsewhere. With our bellies still pressed against the ground, the voice came back on over our radios: "The 51st Mech. is done, gents."

THE REST OF THE NIGHT was spent alternating between struggling to fall asleep and sitting a tense fire watch. Some people say that it's hard to fall asleep in a war zone. To an extent this is true. We were exhausted, and I personally had not slept in two days. But my internal Marine mechanism kept waking me up every thirty minutes. The first time I woke up I was surprised to be in Iraq; for some reason my mind made me think I was somewhere else. When it was my turn for watch, I passed the time trying to figure out if shadows were really moving, and, if so, whether they belonged to an enemy fighter. I scanned the area with my NVGs. The only things in front of me were a few small buildings and miles of desert. Garcia and I switched on and off until dawn.

We were now two days into the invasion. We ran barbed wire across the road to block the only entrance leading into the gas oil separation plant (GOSP), and had interpreters create large signs in Arabic that read, "Road closed. Turn around. U.S. forces will shoot."

A while later, a truck appeared in the distance traveling at a medium speed and heading toward our barbed-wire blockade. It wouldn't stop. The truck swerved in an attempt to go around and through the wire. All the guys on the line opened up, mostly aiming for the tires and engine block. The truck came to a rolling stop and the people inside dashed out, running back the way they'd just come. Because they appeared unarmed, we could not fire on them. But the truck sat there as an example for the Iraqis not to try and cross the line.

A few hours later, another truck came rolling down the road. The vehicle was traveling fast but slowed down when it saw the barbed wire. We thought they would turn around, but they didn't. Instead, they hit the gas and tried to breach the barbed wire. Miguel took a well-aimed shot through his ACOG (Advanced Combat Optical Gunsights) scope at the driver's head. But when he took the shot, the driver turned his head sideways toward the window, and the bullet grazed his ear. The driver jumped out of the truck and surrendered. Some Marines approached the man, and a corpsman patched him up and gave him a cigarette. But without concrete proof of enemy intent, we weren't allowed to detain him, so we let him go.

Although we had shot our rifles, this was not the kind of contact we sought. During the late afternoon we headed north. None of us had fired at the declared enemy. Worse, on our second night of the war, a massive sandstorm struck and temporarily stalled the invasion. Blinding waves of sand slammed us all night. I couldn't believe how violent a sandstorm could be. All you could see was an orange-brown fog. We sat in our position for a good eighteen hours. I would periodically fall asleep only to be awoken by my body twitching in fits of restlessness.

The morning of our third day in war, we loaded up our twelve AAVs and again pushed toward Baghdad. My AAV was toward the front of the column, fourth in line, as I recall. We took turns sleeping inside the trac until it was our turn on air watch. When my time came, I climbed through the left-side of the hole and popped up, exposing myself from the mid-chest up, the typical amount of torso exposure for air watch. The sun was beginning to rise. Up ahead, I could just make out what appeared to be a large town. The streets we were on were flanked by adobe-style buildings that varied between one and three stories tall. Some Iraqis waved, others didn't.

The buildings looked like children's alphabet blocks stacked atop one another in random configurations, heights, and patterns. That makes them hard to patrol, because there isn't one continuous sightline to follow. What's more, there are hundreds of nooks and crannies in which enemy can burrow and hide. My eyes quickly moved from buildings to doorjambs to windows to alleyways. And that's when I heard the sound that accompanies virtually every ambush in Iraq—the whistling of enemy RPGs whizzing through the air.

"They're taking fire in the front!" Birdsong yelled. "RPGs!"

Our column jerked to a stop.

"Contact left! Contact left!"

Enemy fighters began popping out from behind rooftop ledges, walls, and windows. Bullets punched holes in the water cans hanging on the outside of our vehicle.

"Where you at? Where you at?" I whispered to myself while scanning a building with my rifle.

"Nothing. Nothing. Nothing . . . There!"

Up in the window of a three-story building, I could see an Iraqi wearing a white "man dress," firing his AK-47 at our vehicles.

I circled the front sight tip of my rifle around to zero in on him. With my left eye closed, I got my front sight tip centered in the rear sight and focused on his chest. I took a deep breath and pulled the trigger. The round left the barrel and hit him in the chest, knocking him down inside the building. His AK-47 with folding stock tumbled out the window and clanked off ledges.

"Got you, motherfucker!" I said.

Seeing my kill go down like that reminded me that just as he had been in my sights, so too could I be in someone else's. As we'd been constantly reminded, we were now in a 360-degree threat. That meant there were angles and blind spots that anyone—Marines or Iraqis—could exploit.

For example, a guy was popping up and down from behind a wall on the two-story building to the right of the building that housed my first kill. I could see this guy getting off five-shot bursts at my Marine brothers in the front of our column. He had no idea that my position, which was about twenty-five meters away, had given me a perfect shot that was unobstructed by the wall he hid behind. I scanned the length of his body with my rifle while tuning out the sounds of the ongoing firefight.

First I pointed the tip of my rifle at his kidneys.

No, kidneys aren't going to do shit, I thought.

Then I aimed at his rib cage.

No, bullets can be deflected by ribs, I remembered.

Next, I aimed at his head. Some people say headshots are showoff bullshit and are the lowest-percentage shot. But I had no choice; it was my best chance at taking him down with a single shot. I took a deep breath and waited for my natural respiratory pause. I pulled the trigger and felt the recoil go back once. A red blast sprayed out of the enemy's head before his body fell to the roof. One minute later, the short four-minute ambush had been quelled and our AAVs rumbled on.

Our trac drove forward. I looked to the sun. I felt no remorse or sympathy whatsoever for the two men I'd just killed. I know you're not supposed to say things like that; it's not the politically correct, pseudo-sympathetic thing to do. But it's the truth. If anything, I felt *better,* not worse. I had finally become a true Marine. I wasn't going to throw a party over it or anything. Thousands of Americans across numerous generations have punched lead into enemy fighters. I was just doing my job. But it felt good to know that when the moment came, I hadn't frozen up. Still, anyone who says killing another human being doesn't in some way—large or small—change him is a liar. It *does* change something inside you. Not in a fucked-up Travis Bickle/*Taxi Driver* sort of way. But it changes the way you view yourself and the world around you. Irony of ironies, it made me treasure and value life all the more.

We moved down the road like nothing had happened. The only indication that a firefight had taken place were the dead bodies and spent shell casings we left behind. Siler tapped me on the shoulder for his turn at fire watch. I ducked back inside our trac. Most of the men in the trac were asleep or half awake. Tardif and I started talking. We were both exhausted, as was everyone else. Sleep had lost its rejuvenating power. It was more of a nuisance, actually, because you couldn't ever relax enough to fall into a peaceful rest. I didn't know how our trackers were doing it. They had to drive for hours and then man the .50 cals. At least we had the luxury of trying to catch some sleep while not on fire watch. Those guys are golden.

The next morning, we saddled up and pushed north. By now we

had passed the seemingly endless deserts of southern Iraq and had moved into a lush green terrain. We'd been moving all day, stopping only here and there to give friendly Iraqis humanitarian MREs. That evening, we linked up with the 11th Marines, an artillery battery that had been using the area as a temporary headquarters. Their presence made me feel a lot safer. The area was bustling with activity. Vehicles and people scurried around like ants. We now had strength in numbers.

Our company was assigned an area along a road where we were told we could sleep. Since the 11th Marines had the entire area secured, we would only need to provide our own fire watch. This was good news. Maybe now we could finally get some much-needed rest.

I took off my gear except my flak jacket and used my gas mask carrier as a pillow. I was out. Within minutes, however, I was ripped from my sleep by the scariest reveille I ever experienced during my entire time in the USMC.

BOOM! BOOM! BOOM!

The world was exploding. Incoming enemy artillery pounded the ground. My ears were ringing. Guys scrambled. This was not the way I wanted to die—by some anonymous cannon cocker. None of us could tell where the rounds were landing. All we could feel was the concussions. We'd been warned Saddam might resort to gas. Soon the call came.

"GAS! GAS! GAS!"

Anytime an explosion occurred, we'd been told to don and clear. So we did. Huge flashes of light blazed off to our left. The sounds were coming in volleys. I focused on the outline of something until my vision sharpened. It was a howitzer.

I squinted harder and could now see an entire gun line. It was

11th Marines. We had set up so close to the guns that we thought we were being shelled. None of the 11th Marines noticed our embarrassing mistake, thank God. But to this day, I still can't believe that not one Marine saw us sleeping across the street from the damn gun line. It's kind of funny now, but it damn sure wasn't when it happened. Instead, it was an important reminder of how simple miscommunication could mean fratricide.

We moved to another, more quiet area. But after that, who could really sleep? I gave up even trying and instead watched the gun crews work with machine-like precision. Each team had a smooth system in which they loaded the rounds into the breach of the gigantic guns. The shots from each gun fired in perfect synchronization. It was fascinating to watch such skilled teams make grueling and difficult work look so fluid and seamless.

Moving again, we made our way to another area in some tall grass so far away from 11th Marines that we had to set up our own perimeter. Our plans to go on a reconnaissance patrol were canceled when we learned the Iraqis were jamming our radios. So we spent the night in the tall grass. The long green stalks reminded me of the grasses I used to play war in as a kid.

When morning broke, we packed up and moved out. I took first air watch. With the cool wind against my face, I looked forward toward the majestic Iraqi sunrise. We were four days into a war, but the beauty of the sun taking its place in the sky still remained. Same sun, different world.

8

Contact

I don't recommend sleeping in Iraqi landfills.

The reason we were there in the first place, we were told, was to throw off the enemy. The plan was to sleep in the landfill for a single night and move out at sunrise. Plans change. We made the landfill our home for a week. It just so happened that I was on air watch when our trac pulled in.

"Martinez, what's it look like out there?" someone asked.

Everyone in the belly of our trac kept asking how the landfill looked. Visibility was low. Dust had kicked up and was whooshing through the air. Still, from what I could see, the landfill looked about the same as any American landfill—and smelled like one, too.

The ramps dropped and our company made a perimeter before setting into our assigned positions. We started to dig our fighting holes and a horde of flies descended upon us.

"Motherfucker!" I yelled.

Garcia laughed at me until a fly flew straight into his mouth.

"Motherfucker!" he yelled, now sticking his tongue out and scrunching his face.

I gritted my teeth while laughing so as not to eat a fly.

I pulled out my E-tool and put it in an L-position. Garcia took a defensive position. We would take turns digging. I took a hard swing at the ground. Then another, and another, until the head of my E-tool plunged and planted into something solid. I jerked the shovel back hard to dislodge it. Something cracked. A volcano of putrid stench erupted into the air. I crouched down to look closer.

It was a human head.

"What the hell?" I said.

Garcia broke his concentration to the front and looked at my discovery.

"UHHHHH!"

The strangest part was that my E-tool was halfway stuck inside a human head and I wasn't nearly as freaked out as I probably should have been. I yelled over to Staff Sergeant Sikes. He walked over, nose covered, and told me to rebury the head and find a new spot. Garcia helped me bury the half-rotten head, which has got to be the true definition of friendship if ever there was one.

Digging our fighting holes in a landfill proved difficult. With every few swings of the E-tool, we had to stop and clear out the layers of refuse and garbage buried beneath the surface. Worse, the trash had been there so long that it had fused with the ground. We cleared away hypodermic needles, human hair, and every other thing you'd never want to sleep in until finally we had a decent hole. We set ourselves in the fields of fire and took a short rest. The flies were on us like shit. This made those "save the starving children" commercials look like amateur hour. You could swat a half dozen flies by just swinging your hand. I made the mistake of opening something to eat, and within seconds my pouch meal was buzzing. I cursed and threw the wasted meal in back of us about ten yards and buried it.

Garcia and I were standing watch for the two holes on either side of us when something caught my eye. Two partially buried dead bodies lay a few feet in front of us. They had blended in with all the trash. Rigor mortis had already set in, but they hadn't been dead long. We reported the unwelcome discovery but were told to stay in our position because the fields of fire were already set.

The next day, after my squad returned from an eerie security patrol in which we came across a small community of shanties made from garbage, Garcia made another grisly discovery: three more dead bodies, these riddled with bullet holes, lay swarming with flies. Their faces were waxy and discolored. They had each been shot in the back of the head several times, a sign that they may have been executed by Fedayeen Saddam, the most ruthless and loyal of Saddam's forces. By this time in Iraq, we had all seen numerous dead bodies. It had lost its shock value. You always hear about how trauma unit surgeons compartmentalize their emotions from their work. I guess we did the same.

We radioed our third find to Reaper 6, our CO. He wisely put the company on high alert, which we'd already put ourselves on anyhow. Then, fewer than one hundred meters away, Garcia found three *more* dead bodies. *Are we in a landfill or a cemetery?* I thought. Finding dead bodies in an American landfill would have been a major event. Not in Iraq. Our corpsman, who, it must be said, has one of the most kick-ass last names ever—Deathrage (nicknamed "The Rage")—squatted down to get a better look. We again radioed up to Reaper 6 and patrolled on. I wondered what had happened to those people. What events led to their deaths? Who shot them? And what had compelled someone to kill them in such a brutal manner?

When we returned to our hole, word had been passed that it was okay to light fires to keep the flies away. Garcia and I made a fire and took turns eating while the other one stoked the flame and fed it trash. None of us had taken our boots off since the dispersal area back in Kuwait; it had been a week since we'd aired out our feet. A line from the movie *Forrest Gump* popped into my head: Lieutenant Dan tells Forrest and Bubba, "There is one item of G.I. gear that can be the difference between a live grunt and a dead grunt: socks . . . Try and keep your feet dry when we're out humpin'. I want you boys to remember to change your socks wherever we stop." That's actually good advice. A grunt with jacked-up feet is useless. When I finally tugged my boots off my swollen feet, I saw that my bleeding blisters were now showing early signs of "trench foot."

"Garcia," I said, "I'll man my gun. Check your feet."

His were in the same condition—as were most of the company's. Some had it far worse, in fact. Padilla's feet, for example, were missing huge chunks of skin and had bloody craters so deep that he wasn't allowed to go on patrols until they healed. All we could do was cover our feet in powder and slip on fresh socks.

On March 31, 2003, we were told there was no chow. The rumor was that a peace activist group had blocked a ship carrying our food by creating a chain of dinghy boats tied together. The likelihood of such a thing being accurate was almost zero, but it was a creative rumor. Not up to Magana's "J-Lo died" caliber, but a fine effort nonetheless.

As the days passed with no resupply in sight, things started to look grim. Guys were out of food and had already begun resorting to eating humanitarian MREs despite being told not to. When I saw Tardif ripping into one, I gave him shit. "Hey, Marine!" I said in my best officer impersonation. "What do you think you're doing?"

"Shit, I'm eating an MRE," he said.

"Negative, Marine!" I replied. "Those chows are for hungry Iraqis."

Tardif played along.

"What about us?" he said.

"Who gives a damn about you?" I said in a deep voice. "What about the hungry Iraqis? How would it look if you were caught on TV eating a humanitarian chow, huh? You have no discipline! You nasty shitbird!"

We laughed, and soon I sat down and ripped into a humanitarian MRE. The humanitarian MREs were way different from traditional MREs in that they were "culturally appropriate" meals with no pork products and were full of things like lentils and equally gross-tasting foods. But I ate the thing anyway and tried to ration what little water I had left. Our personal canteens were all that remained.

A day later, our sniper team, Shadow 4 (Beltran and Estrada from SOI), helped take our minds off landfill living. After conducting R&S (reconnaissance and surveillance), they returned with intelligence on a nearby enemy military base. That's when we got a mission to raid the base. Lieutenant Maurer gave us our brief: "Okay, we are going to conduct a raid on a military base about 3,000 meters away. The area is reportedly crawling with enemy. They are heavily armed. They have three advantages over us: They have watchtowers, they outnumber us, and they have a tank. We will have no trac support because they will remain in the landfill. We are going to be the point element for the company. 1st and 3rd Squads will cover our flanks. 2nd Squad will be with the breaching team, which will be from 2nd Squad [Hot Rod and Jolly]. 2nd Squad will provide security while the breach team places C-4 charges on a fence that surrounds the base. You know what that means; they will know we are coming. After the breach is blown, it's balls to the wall. We will have lost our element of surprise once the C-4 detonates. It's a good 300 meters of open terrain from the fence to the main buildings of the base. So I don't have to tell you how bad shit can get. Once we're on the objective, our job as a platoon is to establish a stronghold inside the camp that will allow the rest of the company to join us. Any questions?"

Nobody had questions.

The lieutenant took a small piece of paper and drew a layout of the base based on Shadow 4's description and reiterated where he wanted each squad to go. We were given thirty minutes of prep time. I had a pounding headache. I got some Marine Corps M&Ms (800-milligram tablets of Motrin) and swallowed them with the final gulp of water from my canteens. The entire platoon cammied up their faces. We were pumped about our raid. The company got into a tactical formation and patrolled toward the base, stretching out for a couple hundred meters.

About 500 meters from the base we came across a small mud-filled canal. The amount of gear we wore made jumping across it difficult. I made it about three-quarters of the way when my left leg plunged into the stagnant water and sunk down into the thick mud. I used a nearby bush to pull my now-suctioned boot free from the muck.

Once we got to the other side of the canal, I spotted the watch-tower. My heart sank. A man was inside the tower; we'd been spotted. When I looked closer, however, I realized that the man inside the tower had been shot to death and was merely slouched over. I hadn't heard a shot, but Shadow 4 was so good that they very well could have taken him out at such a distance that amid all the sloshing water I might not have heard the gunshot.

We arrived at the breach site as the sun dropped heavy in the Iraqi sky. The company set into position. 2nd Squad and our SMAW team low-crawled to the fence line. 2nd Squad covered Hot Rod and Jolly as they set the explosive charges along two fence posts and made their way back to our position. Once they had decent cover, they detonated the C-4 charges.

"GO! GO! GO!" Tardif yelled.

The fourteen members of 2nd Squad, followed by the rest of 1st Platoon, followed by the entire company, raced through the breach site and secured the immediate area. But by the time we got to the base, it had been abandoned. 1st Platoon set up near two buildings as 2nd Squad cleared them out. When we got inside the buildings, we found large ammunition and weapons caches. Hundreds of RPG rockets, mortars, grenades, and countless 7.62 rounds were strewn about the buildings. Each room also had plenty of AK-47s, RPG launchers, and mortar tubes to put the ammo in motion. We'd narrowly missed the enemy, but it sent a shiver up my spine to think about all this firepower being thrown at us. In the morning, we moved out without blowing the ammo and weapons caches. Several of us thought this was a huge mistake. The rationale was that disposing of the weapons caches would take too much time and deplete resources. This seemed illogical to me, but what did I know? I was just a corporal.

The next morning, we set up shop a few miles from the abandoned military base in a tiny community that looked like something straight out of the Bible. It had mud and hay adobe homes without indoor plumbing and was surrounded by a four-foot adobe wall. Crudely built stables and pens with goats and chickens were scattered throughout the roughly two-acre village. We set up a perimeter and began clearing out the empty community. *Where are all the people in this place?* I thought.

While clearing the community, we discovered a chicken coop with live birds inside. A few of us started joking that we should cook and eat the squawking birds.

"Shit," said Garcia, "I'll prepare them if somebody else knows how to cook them."

Everybody just looked at one another, thinking, *Should we?* We were so hungry we stopped joking around and started figuring out how to get some Iraqi rotisserie chicken. I was a city kid who hadn't learned that bird-neck-wringing trick that farmers know, so instead I volunteered to kill the birds with a Maddox handle (a small pick for digging). Other platoon mates plotted on the best way to cook the birds. Before you knew it, we had an assembly line going. We were finding our inner chefs. Hell, we even stuffed the chicken with a nice rice pilaf from somebody's emergency situation chow. We were really getting into it. Using the last of our water, 1st Platoon and our SMAW gunner attachments boiled the chicken before roasting it over a makeshift fire pit.

While the chicken was cooking, a few of us explored the abandoned community. The rooms had no mattresses or running water— usually just a small chest of drawers to hold all the possessions. In one room, we found some makeup and magazine photos of heavily made-up European and American female models. Evil Western culture had apparently reared its imperialistic, makeup-covered head.

Finally, Dreyer approached with a piece of piping-hot chicken. It had a weird aftertaste, but when you're sleeping in landfills surrounded by dead bodies and haven't eaten in two days, you can handle a strange aftertaste.

That night, with a stomach full of chicken, I went to sleep in my hole, freezing my ass off in the Iraqi night. But a mortar attack startled me awake. The loud explosions prevented me from falling back to sleep. I knew that somewhere out there was an FO (Forward Observer) directing artillery and mortar teams to adjust the trajectory of their rounds to kill us. I spent the rest of the night looking for the FO with my NVGs.

The next morning, we received word that we'd been tasked with supporting an engineer unit that was building refueling stations. After traveling for most of the morning, we reached the area by midafternoon. The company dubbed the area "The Oasis" because of its lush landscape. Palm trees and vibrant, green vegetation covered just about everything in sight. We dismounted and tied in with the rest of the already-established perimeter. Directly in front of our lines ran a small stream. The owners of the large homes to our right stood and watched us from afar as the obligatory digging of holes got under way. The dirt scooped easily, but before we could celebrate, small earth-toned creatures began squirming in the dirt.

"What the hell?" I said.

Garcia looked over the spot I was digging. I'd hit a scorpion nest. Dozens of tiny scorpions were now squiggling in the disrupted nest. Garcia and I checked each other over to make sure neither of us had any scorpions on us. I'd heard that baby scorpions are more dangerous than the adult scorpions because they can't regulate the amount of venom they inject. Down the line Marines were striking all kinds of finds, including snake nests.

The lush surroundings did have some benefits, however. Like water, which we desperately needed. In fact, the next morning brought my first brushing of teeth since the invasion began. I also shaved using water, a great luxury after weeks of dry shaving. But my shaving treat was interrupted by a fuming Dreyer, who ran up with Siler trailing behind.

"Martinez, Siler is being belligerent," said Dreyer.

"What did he do?"

Dreyer then told me how Siler had intentionally ripped his ranger roll off his body after the executive officer (XO) had said to put away sleeping gear.

I looked at Siler. "Is this true?"

Siler indicated that it was. Since Siler was in my squad, it was up to me to do something.

"Well, how do you guys want to handle this?" I asked.

There was no way to handle this administratively. They both wanted to fight out their differences. So I agreed to be the referee. We went to an area right in back of the lines where Terrone and Welsand could maintain watch without pointing their weapons at Dreyer or Siler. The fighters dropped their MOPP suit coats and put on their black leather gloves. (The MOPP suit trousers are kept up with built-in suspenders.) This made the two of them look like characters straight out of Steinbeck's novel *Of Mice and Men*.

The fight itself was pretty comical. I had to break them up three different times because Dreyer kept putting Siler in a death-grip choke hold. The fight ended, they shook hands, and that was that. We got back on line and continued like nothing had happened. There were no hard feelings. It was just the way grunts handled things.

ON THE MORNING OF April 3, 2003, we took our second contact. We were traveling on a highway headed north toward the Euphrates River when, twenty-five meters away, RPGs zipped through the sky and a barrage of enemy gunfire came down on us.

"Contact! Contact!" came the cry over the radio.

The tracs rolled to a stop into the best available fighting positions. The throaty bursts of enemy AK-47s echoed in the air. The sharp punches of our M-16s answered in reply. The guns sounded like they were arguing with each other. Enemy weapons jutted out the windows of the ambush houses that lined the road. Gun smoke was everywhere. Finding targets was easy; they were everywhere, firing down on us from every angle. I aligned my sights with target after target and pulled the trigger again and again. I shot a 40 mm grenade into a house. After the explosion, the shooter ceased firing. Then I shotgunned 40 mm rounds until my grenadier's vest was expended. The only time I broke from firing was to change out empty magazines.

Marine rounds blew off chunks of wall from the ambush houses. My brothers were blazing, but what had me worried was the sound of enemy rounds plinking off our trac. As this thought occurred to me, I saw Tardif, who was standing on the left side of our AAV, move quickly from his firing position, like he was dodging something. I didn't understand his erratic dodges until after we had made it out of the kill zone and down the highway for a quick sit rep (situation report). Nobody from the company had been seriously hurt—the lethal fire our .50 cal. gunners laid down from atop our tracs took care of that—but I noticed scores of dents and scrapes on our AAV from bullets. Most of the packs hanging outside our AAV had been shot several times. The water can that hung in front where Tardif had been standing had also been shot, and the whole left side of the trac was covered with divots and dings from the enemy rounds.

I looked down at Tardif. "Hey, Tardif," I said. "You almost got hit."

"Yeah, I know," he said dryly.

"Shit, man, you lost one of your nine lives."

"Luck of the Irish!" he said, referring to the four-leaf-clover tattoo on his right forearm.

Then I looked at the position where I stood during the firefight. There were fewer impact marks than Tardif's area, but there were enough to make me realize how close I'd come to being shot.

We moved all the way to the Tigris River and took up a defensive position on the riverbank. Baghdad was now just about fifty miles away. Once the line was established, Staff Sergeant Sikes and Lieutenant Maurer ordered 2nd Squad to conduct security patrol. The area we moved through was bright green and thick with overgrown vegetation. While wading through the tall elephant grass with our weapons at the ready, we spied a couple of men wearing white man dresses about 200 meters ahead. As we crept closer, we saw that it was two men accompanied by two women in traditional Middle Eastern attire. Something wasn't right about these guys, we all agreed.

When we got fifty yards away, the two men spotted us and took off in a dead sprint. We tried to chase them, but with all our gear on, we were far too slow. The women stood crying hysterically and clutching their children. Tardif and I shot each other a "What the fuck?" facial expression. He tried to ask the women what was wrong and why they were crying, but communication was futile. Right then, our corpsman, The Rage, yelled out, "Hey guys, come check this out!" On the ground lay two long handmade backpacks, each of which held an SKS assault rifle. The weapons were in immaculate condition and were locked, loaded, oiled, and ready to fire.

"These motherfuckers were going to shoot us but bitched out," said Tardif.

"Looks that way," I agreed.

That was the first inkling I got that Iraq had the potential to devolve into a guerrilla war if we didn't clean house.

When the ladies saw that we had found their men's weapons, they became frantic. With their husbands' attempts to mask their insurgent status now foiled, the women clearly thought we would do to the men what insurgents did to other Iraqis who fled: shoot them in the back as they ran. But we didn't. Birdsong and Garcia slung the beautiful assault rifles across their backs, and we radioed Reaper 6 what had happened. With the threat of retribution gone, the women quickly fell silent. We walked past them without saying a word.

When we got back to friendly lines an hour later, the higher-ups seemed not to care about the precision assault rifles we'd found, and they instructed us to just throw the bolts in the river along with the rest of the rifles. I was surprised by the command's cavalier attitude, and none of us wanted to throw such nice rifles in the river. But orders were orders. So we tossed the dismantled weapons.

OUR GUARD ALWAYS had to be up, even when we were dealing with Iraqi children. Sadly, we had been warned that kids were sometimes used as bait to lure sympathetic Marines in for an ambush or as spotters for targeting and assassinating Marines. Worse, the United Nations says there are a quarter of a million children soldiers in the world.

But throughout my seven months in Iraq, the vast majority of women and children I encountered were peaceful and friendly. In fact, many were downright generous and grateful. I'll never forget the one little kid who wore a Bart Simpson T-shirt while offering Marines cigarettes. There was also a woman who would come out and give dates and homemade flatbread to any Marine who was hungry. We'd been taught to be suspicious of food from locals for fear of poisoning, but I ate flatbread from this wonderfully motherly woman after she ate some too. It was delicious. A war zone might seem like a strange place for such warmth and hospitality, but it was greatly appreciated.

Another thing that seemed out of place were some of the off-the-wall conversations we had. I remember once chatting with Lieutenant Maurer over chow. The lieutenant was a white guy from Tampa, Florida, a great leader, and looked very much the frat boy type. In the course of the conversation, Lieutenant shared that in college he had majored in business finance. The conversation quickly turned to the stock market. Staff Sergeant Sikes joined the conversation. He was an active trader on the New York Stock

Exchange. Somehow, we got on the subject of fast-food franchises and the numerous regulations and bureaucratic red tape that came with owning a Jack in the Box burger joint. Lieutenant Maurer and Staff Sergeant Sikes went back and forth discussing the ins and outs of regulatory constraints on small-business owners. They schooled us about the importance of diversifying one's asset allocations—not the kind of lesson any of us expected to get in the middle of a war.

But warm moments with Iraqis and humorous ones with leaders came to a screeching halt when we got the news that the beloved First Sergeant Smith from Fox Company had died in a firefight. We were speechless. First Sergeant Smith was a former 1st Force operator and had been the first sergeant for Fox Company 2/5. He was also good friends with First Sergeant Bell, aka "Skeletor." He had been an actual grunt and was one of the elite. More than that, he was someone whom everyone in the battalion revered and respected. To hear that a Marine of his caliber and accomplishment was no longer with us was a battalion-wide blow. It was a painful reminder that even the best sometimes meet with a premature death.

The night we learned of First Sergeant Smith's death was the same night we were put on high alert. It was April 7, 2003. We were now near Baghdad, and the closer we got to the "eagle's nest," the fiercer the resistance would be. Republican Guard and packs of Fedayeen Saddam would be spoiling for a fight. Before bed, I pulled fire watch and spent another night second-guessing the shadows that played tricks on the mind.

At sunup, we moved out and traveled late into the afternoon until we arrived at an abandoned Iraqi Army base in the middle of the desert not far from where we had just been when we found out First Sergeant Smith died. Our tracs used the predug Iraqi defilade for their fighting positions. I looked around at the abandoned Iraqi post. Equipment, uniforms, vehicles, weapons, and an array of military effects were scattered all over the ground for hundreds of yards. Whoever left this place left in a hurry and didn't want to be identified as soldiers.

My fire team was chosen to clear out the area 180 degrees to the front of our trac. We did a quick gear check and set off in a wedge formation. We cleared a labyrinth of trenches and fighting holes while checking for booby traps. The precision and fortification of the holes and trenches freaked us out a little bit; they were impeccable and sophisticated. We'd been told that the Iraqi military force was mediocre, but this was not the work of amateurs.

We exited the trenches and investigated a mobile lab that resembled a large truck trailer. The inside of the trailer looked like something you would find in a university chemistry lab, complete with tubes and beakers. Garcia and I exited the vehicle quickly for fear of contamination and rejoined Birdsong and Miguel outside. As we prowled through the abandoned enemy base, I noticed an anti-aircraft (AA) gun. It was loaded and ready to go. We all looked at one another; we had been told that most AA guns had already been eliminated. Birdsong, Garcia, Miguel, and I then unloaded the 10-inch-long 30 mm rounds. For a split second, I thought about putting a grenade in the gun's feed tray to render it inoperable, but something told me I'd probably get in trouble if I did.

We surveyed the many military vehicles inside the enemy base. Some had huge bullet holes in them, while others were in pristine condition. This base had everything—except rifles, that is. We never found a single one on our entire patrol. The Iraqis took every rifle with them.

When we got out 200 meters from the rest of the company, Garcia, our point man, gave the hand and arm signal for the patrol to freeze in our footsteps. He then motioned for the squad to get down. Through nonverbal signals, he communicated that he had seen two, possibly three, guys rummaging through a truck to our front. Without speaking, I signaled Miguel to use his ACOG scope to recon the area in question. Miguel low-crawled over to a concealed position and fed information back to me via personal radio.

Sure enough, one hundred yards from our position were two guys pilfering through a large seven-ton truck. I told Miguel we needed to check it out and see who they were and what they were up to. I briefed the fire team on the "scheme and maneuver" before we moved tactically from concealed position to concealed position. The men had no clue we were there. When we got closer, I could see that they weren't militants or soldiers, but instead hungry Iraqis scavenging for food. When we got right up on them, I used my most commanding voice: "U.S. Marines."

The startled men jumped back. When I looked in their eyes, I could see that they were scared out of their minds. I held up a piece of paper on which the word "Friend" was printed in Arabic. The men seemed relieved but still extremely nervous. One of the men started speed-talking and frantically pointing at the food he found. I pointed to my stomach and then back up at them. They smiled. That's when I noticed that one of the men was missing his tongue. I had him open his mouth and looked at the crudely cut stub. The other man explained in rough, broken English that people in Saddam's regime had cut out his tongue.

"Saddam. Bad word. Saddam," the man said while making chopping and cutting motions with his hands.

My heart went out to the men and those like them who had suffered under such a brutal tyrant and regime. The dead Iraqis in the landfills were powerful symbols. But for some reason, standing in front of a living, breathing Iraqi who was a walking embodiment of Saddam's torturous thirty-year reign had an even more powerful effect on me. Here was a man whose rights of free speech—indeed, of *any* speech—had been severed from him.

I gave the men some of my food and told them not to come back around here. They just nodded their heads at whatever I said. I knew they couldn't understand me, but they had reminded me of something more powerful than words could express: The rights we take for granted are the hope and envy of others. I motioned to the men that they were free to leave. They raced off with the food.

After that little house of horrors, we patrolled back toward the company and received the best news since the war began: With the threat of NBC attacks minimized, we were told we would no longer need to wear our MOPP suits. The entire platoon rejoiced. Without hesitation, I unzipped my MOPP top and threw it on the ground with glee. I then unbuckled the suspenders and ripped off my MOPP trousers both legs at once. When the air hit my body it felt like I'd walked into a refrigerator. My entire uniform was stuck to my body and I looked like I'd been swimming. I looked around and my brothers were ripping off their MOPP suits with a happiness seldom seen in grunts.

By nightfall, we had received orders to move to the "eagle's nest," so the next morning we saddled up and headed for Baghdad. When it was my turn to take air watch for our AAV, I could see Baghdad off on the horizon, about twelve miles away. Ambushes were imminent. I loaded a 40 mm grenade in the breach of my M-203 and continued scanning the area.

When we reached our destination in Baghdad, the area was surprisingly jungle-like, complete with a lush green rolling knoll dotted with houses. It didn't fit with the surroundings. We dismounted and Lieutenant Maurer briefed us during a "key leaders meeting."

"Okay, guys, here's the situation. This is a hostile area and contains a large amount of irregular fighters and Republican Guard. We have been tasked to take them out." He paused and looked around at each of us. "We are going to conduct a contact patrol."

A contact patrol is the most coveted of the infantry patrols. Few grunts will ever go on a contact patrol, even in a time of war. This was a once-in-a-lifetime opportunity, we knew immediately. A contact patrol is only ordered in the most dangerous of zones and all but ensures "contact." Marines on a contact patrol become human wrecking balls, leaving maximum carnage in their path, as any person encountered, armed, is to be considered hostile and "killed at will."

Lieutenant Maurer gave us the rules of engagement (ROE).

"You are to take out anybody displaying any type of aggression toward U.S. forces. Anybody in the area is considered hostile. Contact is imminent. I repeat: Contact is imminent. Any questions?"

When the brief ended, De La Fuente, who was one of 2nd Squad's fire team leaders, Tardif, and I returned to the squad to report the good news. The squad cheered and immediately began prepping for the patrol. Our SMAW gunners loaded a rocket in the SMAW, the machine gunners put in a "starter belt" of ammunition, and I double-checked my fourteen magazines. Following gear inspection Lieutenant Maurer gave us the order to "step off," with 1st Platoon being the point element for the patrol and 2nd Squad the "tip of the spear."

We entered the dense jungle. Five minutes into the patrol, we began seeing hundreds of Iraqi Army uniforms scattered across the ground. Weapons by the dozens sprinkled the ground. We then spotted AA guns. This was the perfect spot for them because of the dense trees overhead. Even in aerial photos the weapons would go undetected.

The soles of our boots tread over the many uniforms that carpeted the jungle floor. Moving through the jungle, we passed large weapons caches. Each cache was massive—fifty feet by fifty feet. Most of what we saw included explosives for artillery and missiles. On the sides of the boxes, the word JORDAN was printed in yellow letters. "Jordan" is a friend of the United States with whom we often share intelligence. Off to our left stood a huge house in the distance. I kept an eye on it. We had patrolled 200 yards. With every footstep I could feel my heart thump.

That's when we walked up on a man wearing green Iraqi Army pants and a white T-shirt. He took off like he had seen a ghost. Garcia tried to get him in his sights, but the man disappeared into the tree line. *Shit,* I thought, *that was probably their LPOP* (listening post observation post). Using hand and arm signals, I told Garcia to take the patrol to a run pace. He ran off with the rest of the squad following. In the event the man was trying to lure us into an ambush, we took a different route than he had.

After five minutes of running, we reached a large adobe wall, approximately five feet tall and beige in color. Using hand and arm signals, I instructed my team to get low. I scanned the length of the wall. It went as far as I could see in both directions. Weapons and ammo caches lay near the wall. Tardif came on over the radio net. I explained what was going on. He wanted to know what was on the other side of the wall, so I peeked over and saw some buildings, a two-lane road, and more jungle across the road. Tardif instructed us to jump the wall.

Garcia went first, followed by Miguel, Birdsong, and then me. When I cleared the wall, a man with an AK-47 strapped to his back and wearing green Iraqi Army pants and a white T-shirt revved up his motorcycle and rode straight at us. I could tell as he came toward us it was the same man we had stumbled upon in the jungle. We opened fire, but he only gunned the motorcycle harder. The engine screamed—*WEEEEEENNNNNN!*

As he passed us, our rounds tore into his back. His bike began to wobble. He skidded across the street before crashing into the tree line opposite the side we had just come from.

The rest of the squad had now made it over the wall and joined us on the other side. With our attention focused on the motorcycle gunman, we hadn't noticed the car now barreling straight for us. We jumped out of the way to avoid being hit and opened withering fire on our attackers. The rounds turned the car's rear windshield white with cracks until the riddled car veered off in the same direction as the motorcycle attacker before wrapping around a tree.

"LOOK!" someone yelled. "Another one!"

I whipped my head around and saw a second car starting toward us. This driver apparently changed his mind, because the car U-turned and sped off. I looked back over at the car we had shot up. The now-bloodied passenger fled the wrecked vehicle and disappeared into the jungle. Miguel and I cautiously approached the vehicle to confirm that the driver was dead. He was. And his fleeing accomplice had left a large blood trail through the jungle, meaning that he was as good as dead. I glanced at the car's backseat. There sat a collection of AK-47s. The trunk had sprung partly open and contained homemade explosive devices.

As we walked back to the squad, who were in the middle of the road, another car came blazing down the road, headed right for us. Oddly, this car slammed to a stop and then started approaching slowly. After a few moments, the driver slammed the gas and shot toward us like an arrow. The passenger had an AK-47 in his hands. Tardif gave the command to open up. With our SMAW team on the right side of the road and the machine gunners on the left, our firepower gnarled the car up like a tin can. When it rolled to a stop, Tardif called a cease-fire. The lieutenant ordered us to jump back over the wall and continue up through the jungle to protect the rest of the company's left flank.

Once on the other side of the wall, we moved into an area of the jungle that was not as dense, and we saw looming in the distance a soaring tower that resembled the Seattle Space Needle. The structure was actually part of an amusement park called Baghdad Island. But I found nothing "amusing" about the structure. In my mind, I pictured my chest in the crosshairs of a terrorist sniper scope. The tower dominated the landscape, and with each step, it became bigger and bigger.

We crossed the land bridge that took us onto Baghdad Island and conducted a long patrol to the amusement park. Along the way, we passed numerous buildings and billboards of Saddam that had since been vandalized. We entered the amusement park through its main entrance. We'd left a trail of bodies in our wake. The contact patrol was complete. Cars full of Iraqis were busy looting the park. Some offered us freshly looted food, but we didn't take any.

We cleared the buildings and rooms inside the park with few surprises. But when we got to the main complex of buildings, inside was nothing I would expect to see at an amusement park. The buildings housed laboratories with all kinds of chemicals, tubes, beakers, lab coats, and goggles. As before, I didn't want us to be in those labs any longer than we had to because God only knows what chemicals we were coming in contact with. As for the tower, Shadow 4 (Golf Company's snipers) took control of it and used their aerial vantage point to cover us until we moved out the following day. We were, however, mortared that night.

A FEW DAYS AFTER the contact patrol, we linked up with the rest of Regimental Combat Team 5 (RCT-5), which included all of 5th

Marines, at Baghdad University. On the way to the university, our tracs started jerking forward and stopping, jerking forward and stopping. We wanted to know what the hell was going on. As it turned out, the trackers had accidentally driven into a minefield and were trying to retrace their moves to extract us without detonating any mines. I kept waiting for the bottom of the trac to explode and send shrapnel through our bodies. After about an hour and a half of awkward maneuvering, we got out of the minefield unscathed.

The entire RCT-5 had assembled and was staying at Baghdad University. But much of our time was spent out on long patrols through downtown Baghdad. During one such patrol, we passed by the area where the first bombs had been dropped on the night of the invasion. Even though several targeted buildings had been demolished, much of the city still bustled with activity. In fact, on several occasions, we had to patrol through bumper-to-bumper traffic.

On one patrol, we were tasked with raiding a Special Republican Guard barracks. After some tense preparations and dynamic entries, we realized that the four-story barracks had been abandoned. The rooms were just like any barracks you would find back at Camp Pendleton, with uniforms, gear, and personal effects strewn about. On the fourth floor, we entered a large room that had been the commander's office. When I stepped inside, the first thing I noticed were the hundreds of blood slides all over the floor. A few microscopes sat on some nearby tables. On the leader's desk sat a large box of CAT scan images along with boxes brimming with medical equipment. That's when Egleston stumbled upon something that— no matter how hard I've since tried—I've been unable to shake from my memory.

He walked up to me and said, "I think you should see this. But before you see what's inside, I have to warn you that what you're about to see will be seared in your mind forever."

Egleston handed me a photo binder. When I cracked it open, my jaw dropped. There in front of me were the most horrifying images of experiments being performed on newborn and infant children. Picture after picture, page after page, the binder was filled with the most extreme deformities and experimental mutations one could imagine. One baby had an eye that was shifted toward the middle of its head.

"What the hell is going on in this country?" I said.

Egleston just shook his head and handed me a second binder. It was just as bad as the first. Toward the end of the binder were pictures of men in white lab coats injecting needles into the stomach of a pregnant woman who was howling in agony. I couldn't handle any more. I slammed the binder shut. Egleston ended up giving the photo binders to our lieutenant as valuable pieces of intelligence.

When we made it to 1st Squad's position, most of the Marines had their attention on some vehicles across the water. I squatted down with my Marine brothers and watched as some Iraqi men were busy loading weapons and ammunition onto some nearby trucks. I asked why they hadn't shot them yet and the answer I received blew my mind. My platoon mates said the XO (who was with us) had denied their request to fire on the men because there was insufficient evidence that the men were hostile. So there they stood, loading weapons and ammunition that would probably be used to kill and injure U.S. troops down the road. The men shot us a defiant look and then showed us the bottoms of their shoes, a cultural statement meaning that they thought we were the scum of the earth. They kept on taunting us, secure in the knowledge that higher-ups had tied our hands behind our backs.

The massive looting you probably remember seeing on television continued unchecked. Whether in stores or on the streets, everything was being looted. Later that evening, we patrolled back to the university, finding loaded RPGs along the roads. As we patrolled, the one thing that made the hairs on the backs of our necks stand up was when the "Prayer Call" sounded through the city's PA system. Everything came to a halt as an eerie voice boomed across the city. There was only one word I could make out. No matter who was conducting the prayer, or how he chose to deliver it, nearly every forty-five seconds one word would resurface, time and time again: "jihad."

9

By the Grace of God

On-the-ground intelligence reports had been deemed credible and good. They indicated that Fedayeen Saddam fighters were massing just north of our position in a large town called Al Tarmiya. Saddam Hussein was considered likely to be in the area. On the morning of April 12, 2003, Golf Company was tasked to investigate the intelligence reports.

We loaded into our AAVs and made the forty-five-minute ride to the edge of town. 3rd Squad was sent to conduct a recon of the entrance to the city while the rest of our platoon waited nervously. After a tense ten minutes, two RPG shots broke the silence. The all-too-familiar whistling sound of several RPGs echoed through the air. Two RPGs had smacked against 3rd Squad's AAV, scoring direct and immobilizing hits on their vehicle. Luckily, most of the Marines inside had already gotten out and begun reconnaissance along the roads. But the three-member AAV crew—the gunner, the driver, and the mechanic—weren't so lucky. The driver had his calf muscle all but sheared off the bone, and the gunner and mechanic were riddled with shrapnel. What sucked was that we weren't there; our trac had yet to cross over the bridge leading into the city—which had turned into an ambush zone. This was the scene we were met with when we finally got the okay to reinforce our ambushed 3rd Squad brothers. The events that unfolded during the next four hours would forever change our lives.

ALL EIGHTEEN OF US sat breathing deeply and pressed against one another, shoulder-to-shoulder, in the dark and claustrophobic confines of our squad's AAV. Rolling across the bridge and into the city where our 3rd Squad brothers were getting pummeled by terrorists, our tracs quickly became tin cans in a shooting gallery. At first, the plinks came in ones and twos. But once the enemy locked in on us, the bullets hitting our AAV sounded like a Vegas slot machine that had just hit jackpot—like an endless stream of coins clinking against a metal plate. We had made our way to the ambush site.

"They're getting hit up the road!" someone yelled. "We've *got* to dismount!"

Our AAV rolled to a halt. The ramp dropped. Sunlight flooded our vehicle.

"Go! Go! Go!"

The smoke and the smell of gunpowder made it hard to breathe. RPGs screamed over us. As soon as our boots hit the ground, we could feel the earth shake from the impact of enemy mortar rounds. Our boots had barely left the ramp when an enemy mortar shell smacked the ground nearby. I slammed to the ground. With the left side of my sweat-covered face mashed against the dirt, I noticed a U.S. military–issue Beretta 9 mm with a broken lanyard lying on the ground. I grabbed it and stuffed it in my right cargo pocket for later use. The sounds of gunfire, rockets, and enemy fighters screaming in Arabic were deafening. I rolled over on my stomach toward Tardif.

"We're sitting ducks here!" I yelled. "Screw this! Let's move and kill some terrorists!"

We sprung up off the ground and charged uncovered down into a field of tall elephant grass toward a series of adobe-style buildings and homes. The rest of 2nd Squad followed. Fedayeen fighters popped up in windows and out of spider holes to shoot at us. We returned fire. They had new, well-maintained AK-47s and high-quality RPG launchers, and they wore all-white ninja-style terrorist uniforms that covered their faces.

The enemy rounds were now coming so close I could feel the heat and the snaps of the rounds passing my ears. There is no logical explanation for how we were getting past all this stuff. It was like swimming in a school of jellyfish and not getting stung. It wasn't skill or technique or luck. It was the grace of God.

Our squad clustered about two hundred yards to the right of the ambush site. Each squad was comprised of two fire teams, a machine-gun team, and a SMAW team. I was the leader of first fire team. Tardif huddled us together and gave us our objectives. My fire team was to go house-to-house and clear each structure of the terrorists within. The plan was to use the SMAW gunners to blow a hole through the eight-foot-tall adobe walls that surrounded each house. We would then race across the street and run through the smoldering hole before entering each house and eliminating the Fedayeen inside.

Tardif and the SMAW team got in position to blast a hole through the first home's surrounding wall. I was across the street, a stone toss away from Tardif, taking shots at the many targets of opportunity materializing in windows. The heat was insane. Sweat ran down our faces like somebody had poured water over our heads. The only relief from the sun were the plumes of smoke that sometimes whisked in front of it. Between popping off shots at the enemy, I could see 3rd and 1st Squads clearing houses. A wave of gratitude came over me. This was what we'd come to do. It felt like the greatest privilege to be doing it finally.

I looked back over at Tardif and the SMAW team. They were seconds from taking the shot. Right then a terrorist sat up in some nearby bushes and lobbed a grenade. The explosive arced through the air and literally bounced off of Tardif's shin.

"Grenade!" Tardif yelled, as he jumped for cover.

Jolly and Hot Rod scurried into a small ditch.

I felt helpless watching it unfold.

"NOOOOOOO!" I yelled.

Shrapnel ripped into Tardif's leg. He tried to stand up but fell over. Tardif was down.

The terrorist who threw the grenade was now sprinting away.

"You bastard!" I yelled.

I aimed my M-16 at the running terrorist who'd just nearly blown up my friend's leg and shot him down. Jolly and Hot Rod rushed over to check on Tardif before shooting at insurgents appearing in the tree line. We didn't have any corpsmen with us, but Miguel was medic trained. I glanced down from shooting and saw Tardif's shin and thigh bone peeking through his flesh wound. He was bleeding profusely. Miguel remained calm and cool and went to work on Tardif, whose face was now white. I thought he was going to bleed out and die.

With no command, the rest of our squad got "on line" with me like a firing squad and began emptying their magazines at the terrorists who had gotten our squad leader. More Fedayeen popped up from hiding places and returned fire at our line. Shooting on line is a big no-no. It's considered John Wayne shit, the kind of thing that can get a whole squad wiped out if the enemy sprays a traversing line of fire. But we didn't give a fuck. Charioello, our M-240 machine gunner, was on line, too. The power of an M-240 requires that it be fired using a tripod, but Charioello was spraying the gun from his hip.

"Get some!" one Marine yelled.

Our rounds sent the attackers' bodies jerking left and right. But they weren't going down easy. One of us landed a shot to one terrorist's head, splitting his skull open and exposing pieces of brain.

The Fedayeen hiding behind trees started retreating. When they ran, we mowed them down. I still remember hearing their cries of agony. Later we'd discover why these bastards wouldn't go down easy. But at the time I thought to myself, *What is this?* Night of the Living Dead?

With the resilient attackers eliminated and Tardif down and fading, I was next in line to assume leadership of the squad. The whole squad looked at me. "What next?" someone asked.

"Three-sixty around Tardif," I replied.

Everyone spread out and created a loose, ringlike perimeter around Tardif. Miguel was still working on Tardif. He took out his knife and started prying the burning shards of shrapnel out of Tardif's leg. I could smell his burnt flesh. I knelt down and grabbed Tardif's hand and looked at his face. He kept fading in and out. He couldn't speak. His eyes swirled around in his head.

"It's going to be okay, dawg," I said. "You're going to be fine. Hang in there. We're going to get you the hell out of here."

Tardif was doing everything he could to hold back the waves of pain. The scene was beginning to make me dizzy. Watching Tardif writhing in agony and yet still displaying the face of leadership was something I don't think I'll ever forget. But the moment was short-lived. The terrorists saw us tending to our injured leader and resumed raining fire down on us, this time from a house behind us. A volcanic rage unlike anything I've ever felt erupted inside me.

I radioed on the clogged net that Tardif had been hit. Chatter stopped and a silence fell over the net. A voice came on and said they would try to arrange a medevac.

I then heard another voice, this one behind me. It was Tardif.

"I'm not going to medevac until the mission is complete," he said.

Seconds later, he passed out from blood loss. I had two Marines sling his arms around their necks and lug him around until the medevac pickup point was established. In the meantime, we had houses to clear and payback to deliver. I turned to "Alf" (De La Fuente, 2nd fire team leader).

"Don't let anyone enter that house once we [1st fire team] are in," I said. "If you see anyone try to go in or out, shoot them." Alf nodded affirmative. Leaving men outside a house ensures that no one goes in or out and, in the worse-case scenario of you dying inside, allows your men to jump in and avenge your death.

The house we were about to enter had no adobe wall surrounding it. So Garcia, Birdsong, Miguel, and I ran across the yard under enemy fire and made a dynamic entry. The second we entered the house, we were in contact with enemy fighters. It was many of them versus only four of us. The enemy were so close that when we shot them blood splattered the walls. The other terrorists were spread throughout the house—hidden in different rooms. We didn't know which rooms they were in or how many terrorists there were, but we could hear them yelling to one another in Arabic.

Gunshots inside the house were amplified to what seemed like a hundred times their normal sound. Every room we entered on the first floor contained at least one terrorist. We were dropping body after body, often just a few feet away from us. Sweat soaked my sleeves. We crept up the stairs. My ears were ringing. All I could hear were the sounds inside me, like swallowing and breathing, and the muffled yells of terrorists and my teammates. I remember feeling that with each stair my boots touched, my heartbeat quickened. We couldn't know what lay in wait for us on the second floor.

"Over there!" I heard Birdsong yell.

We blasted the terrorist and cleared the room.

After we busted into the next room and eliminated more enemy, I stopped to look down at the dead bodies and around the room we were standing in. It was a kitchen, complete with a sink and a running refrigerator. Scattered on one of the countertops were vials of adrenaline, syringes, and *khat* (pronounced "cot"), a drug similar to PCP that gives users a surge of energy and strength. That's when it clicked: Tardif's zombie-like attacker hadn't gone down easily because he was jacked up on *khat* and adrenaline. These guys were the real deal. They'd come to fight and die.

After checking for booby traps, I opened the refrigerator to see whether they were hiding weapons inside. They weren't, but there, in the middle of the refrigerator, was a sealed, unopened bottle of spring water (*khat* produces intense thirst).

"Okay, here's what's next," I said. "We're going to clear this house all the way to the roof. Okay?"

Everyone nodded.

We cautiously made our way to a second-story balcony, where we came in contact with terrorists who were in the backyard. They ran behind a cow and started shooting at us, but their hiding place did no good. We immediately opened up, killing both the cow and the men. After lobbing two grenades up onto the roof to clear or wound any hiding enemy, I rushed to the top of the house, with Birdsong, Miguel, and Garcia following close behind. I'd never been prouder of my fire team; they stayed cool and methodical through it all.

Up on the roof, two minutes of peace had passed when suddenly the house across the way erupted with enemy gunfire. The four of us dropped, hugged the roof, and returned fire.

With the house now cleared all the way to the roof, and with the radio net clogged, I yelled down from the roof for the SMAW team and machine gunners to come up. When they arrived, I instructed the SMAW team to take two shots, one directly at the building in front of us and another to blow a hole in the wall surrounding the house from which the enemy were shooting at us. Our machine gunners opened up while the SMAW gunners took their shots. The first shot made a direct hit in the middle of the three-story house, and the second shot scored a perfect breach. But the enemy fighters inside just kept firing at us.

We got down off the roof and met back up with Alf's fire team, which had to defend its position many times while we were clearing the house. I also saw the injured Tardif. It took one more look at his ghost face and whirling roulette marble eyes to further stoke my rage. But before I could say anything, the house across the street started lighting us up again with gunfire. The entire squad returned fire as we penetrated the smoldering wall. Even if we could run across the street and somehow avoid the enemy snipers and fighters popping up all around us, we'd still be sorely outnumbered inside the second house. The house we'd just cleared turned out to be fifteen of them versus four of us. But what else were we going to do? So we ran at the enemy.

Running across the street and into the hole in the wall was the equivalent of sprinting through highway traffic blindfolded. Enemy rounds smacked the ground around us. We returned fire as best we could while sprinting and ran through the hole in the wall and into the house's front yard. Enemy fighters popped up out of fighting holes like gophers. We took them out quickly. Behind them was a small guesthouse with five terrorists inside alternating between loading and shooting at us.

A few slender palm trees were the only features inside the yard to hide behind, so I jumped behind one of them. The rest of the squad entered the house. A swarm of gunfire whizzed past both sides of my tree trunk. My eyes darted over at Gardner, a white, six-foot Oklahoman, and Jaramillo. Neither of them was from our squad but had come to help with Tardif and offer reinforcement, since we were catching the most hell at that particular point in the firefight. They were both about seven meters to my left. I was glad to see they both made it through safely. But pinned behind palm trees was nowhere we wanted to be. You never want to slow your offensive.

Up overhead, Cobra helicopters whirled on their way to strafe roads and buildings. When the helos passed, the palm fronds on our trees swayed. As the gun battle inside the house raged on, I glanced behind me at the wall we'd just burst through. The sight made my heart jump. The only portion of the wall not riddled with enemy bullets was a narrow twenty-four-inch patch that mirrored the outline of my palm tree trunk. The enemy was now less than fifty feet away. The guesthouse-turned-bunker facing us was filled with fully armed shooters. I began firing round after round of 40 mm at the bunker. Some of the rounds almost made it into the small window. But I couldn't get a steady shot, because if I stayed exposed, I'd get killed. That's when I heard a break in the action; the enemy gun from the guesthouse bunker had jammed. I jumped out from behind my tree and charged the bunker while Gardner, Garcia, and Jaramillo laid down suppressive fire. Halfway to the bunker, I heard the enemy AK-47 reengage and resume firing.

I was stranded.

If I could have mashed the pause button at that instant of my life, it was the only time I was absolutely *certain* I was going to die. Not "thought" I was going to die, or "worried" I might die, but *knew* it. I turned to break contact and braced for my worst fear: getting shot in the back. Getting shot in the back is the worst way for a Marine to die, because it means he was in retreat. Nothing gets pounded into a grunt more than the phrase "Marines never retreat!" It's the worst way to go out. And had I died, I would have considered it a disgraceful and shameful death.

I started sprinting back to a different palm tree some twenty-five yards away. My back was a bull's-eye. On the way back, I noticed an enemy RPG launcher on the ground. To this day, I can't fully explain why I did what I did next: I snatched up the weapon, even though the motion slowed me down and gave the enemy more time to shoot me. Most troublingly, I didn't have a clue how to fire an RPG. But for whatever reason, I picked it up. And for whatever reason, I survived. Now I was in possession of a foreign weapon that I'd never held and had not the slightest idea how to use.

I took cover behind another tree and looked the weapon over. I'd seen them in movies and pictures, but we were never trained how to use enemy weapons. I fumbled with the rocket until it snapped firmly into place. I thought that if I could just somehow figure out how to fire the damn thing, I could destroy the building and free up my brothers. Plus—and I'd be lying if I didn't admit it—I loved the idea of shooting these bastards with their own damn weapon.

I popped out from behind my palm tree.

Squeeze.

Nothing.

I reloaded the rocket, checked the sights, and put it back up on my shoulder again before exposing myself from behind the tree a second time.

Squeeze.

Nothing again.

"Motherfucker!" I muttered.

I started to wonder whether there was a *reason* this stupid thing had been tossed onto the battlefield; maybe it was a dud. That's when the launcher's dual-trigger system caught my eye. If it didn't work this time, I was done fooling with the thing.

No sooner had I exposed myself and gotten into a kneeling firing position than I heard Gardner get hit in the ribs. Gardner's screams sounded like someone getting his arms sawed off. His body collapsed to the ground. He was seven yards away, lying in an expanding pool of deep-red blood.

The Fedayeen zeroed in on his body. Their rounds punched the dirt around him. Gardner's face turned as white as Tardif's had. Blood was pouring out of his mouth, along with gargling sounds. Later we'd learn that he'd been paralyzed from the waist down, but at the time, all we knew was that if we didn't do something fast, another round would find and kill him.

I thought, *If I'm going to fire this thing, I better do it now, because if I don't, they're going to kill Gardner.*

I pointed the RPG back at the terrorists, aimed at the structure, braced for the kickback, and squeezed the trigger. The rocket zoomed across the yard, tearing through the bunker and killing two of the five shooters inside. Most important, the blast bought us a much-needed ten- to fifteen-second break in the action that gave my teammates the time to drag Gardner out of the line of fire.

But even as our guys were scrambling to get Gardner to safety, the three surviving terrorists began firing on the half-dead Gardner and the Marines struggling to drag him to safety.

Something inside me snapped. I went primal.

I ran directly for the enemy bunker, firing my M-16 as Garcia and Jaramillo laid covering fire. When I got fifteen meters from the terrorists who'd paralyzed our brother, the bolt on my rifle locked to the rear; I was out of ammo. I dropped my weapon, which hung from a sling around my body, and prepped a hand grenade while running the final seven meters. I could hear the shooters yelling in Arabic. They ducked down behind their bunker wall and blindly sprayed rounds out of the window.

When my body slammed against the outer wall of their bunker, I threw a grenade as hard as I could into the open window and stood with my back against the wall, waiting for the blast. The concussion from the explosion jolted me forward. A pink mist and body parts flew past me. There had been no outlet for the explosion to go any- where. It was like those guys got put in a blender.

I wasn't sure whether I was alive or dead. It was the most surreal feeling I have ever experienced. My ears had liquid running out of them, and my head ached. I was silent and calm. So was the yard. There were body parts all around me. Two of the bastards who'd shot Gardner lay mutilated on the ground in front of me. I glanced down. Their intestines, slathered in blood, were hanging outside their stomachs.

I reloaded my M-16 and walked behind the blown-up structure. I turned the corner and something moved. Lying on the ground was a severely wounded Fedayeen fighter with an AK-47. As he drew his weapon into a shooting position, I fired four shots—two to the head and two to the chest.

Seconds later, Garcia ran up to me.

"Holy shit!" he said. "Did you see what you did to those guys?"

I was exhausted—more tired than I'd ever been before. I don't know if I ever really replied.

Thankfully, the rest of the company had been monitoring the battle over the radio and had called in an AAV and medevac helo for Gardner and Tardif. Both were still alive, but fading. Doc Bunstone came in the medevac AAV to administer treatment until they could be airlifted out of the mess we were in. When our guys hooked up with the AAV and began loading them into the emergency vehicle, three enemy fighters jumped out of some nearby bushes and began firing. We cut them down in a brief two-minute firefight.

The AAV rushed away as we engaged the enemy. As it turned out, we were standing in the exact spot where Tardif had initially been hit; we could see his now-dried blood on the ground. I glanced several meters in front of us at the Fedayeen fighters whom we'd killed when we were all firing on line. I thought to myself, *So this is combat.* We bounded back the two hundred yards to where the rest of 1st Platoon was. When we got back to the original ambush site, 1st and 3rd Squads now had a stronghold.

That's when I realized I was missing Miguel. My heart dropped to my stomach; I feared he'd been taken as a POW. I alerted Staff Sergeant Sikes of the situation and asked if I could reenter the area we'd just come from. Staff Sergeant Sikes okayed my request, so our squad loaded up with ammo and prepared for a running firefight to look for Miguel. But before we stepped off, we were informed that Miguel was safe inside the medevac trac and was helping keep Gardner alive. I took a deep breath of relief.

We moved out from the area, using tactical movements, staying on alert for ambushes, and firing all the while. When we crossed back over the bridge leaving the town, the gunfire stopped. The area grew silent, almost as if the firefight had never happened. As the company prepared to move back to Baghdad University, some high-speed, low-drag troops, more than likely Army Special Forces bad-asses, passed right in front of us in a tricked-out Humvee— likely to collect intelligence or chase down whoever they were after.

We rolled on toward Baghdad. Our ears were ringing so loud that we had to yell at one another just to be understood.

When we pulled into Baghdad University, the ramps dropped and we exited. The rest of the battalion stood there looking at us with mystified faces. We wrote after-action reports (AARs). Lieutenant Maurer collected the documents from our platoon and said he was proud of each and every one of us. He was always a gracious and complimentary leader. He made a point of giving me special praise for what he had heard I had done, which made me feel uncomfortable.

When we were allowed to rest, I asked Miguel how Gardner had looked before the helo airlifted him. Miguel just shook his head with a grim look on his face. He said he had to slap Gardner every so often so he wouldn't slip into shock. Then I asked about Tardif. Miguel said he, too, was bad off and barely able to speak. The massive blood loss had severely weakened him.

I called a squad meeting and told everyone how proud I was of each of them and that I would write each of them up for at least a NAM (Navy and Marine Corps Achievement Medal) with a V for Valor.

"As long as I'm with you guys, I will never fear for my life," I told them. "The tactical precision displayed out there today makes me *know* we could make it out of anything the enemy has to throw at us. I want you guys to know that it's an honor and a privilege to be your squad leader. I'd go into the depths of hell with each one of you."

Afterward, I went to get my pack off the side of the AAV. When I did, I glanced over at the pack hanging next to mine. It was Tardif's. I said a silent prayer and asked God to allow him to live and to somehow spare Tardif's leg. I then prayed that Gardner could somehow hang on and live. Moments later, Staff Sergeant Sikes said he thought we needed to divvy up Tardif's and Gardner's gear.

Many of the Marines in our platoon could use it, since they had ruined or lost gear during previous firefights and movements.

"I think Tardif will be back," I responded.

Staff Sergeant Sikes looked at me like I was crazy. He took Tardif's pack off the side of the AAV and gave the gear to those who needed it the most (which was the right thing to do). Nowack, a SMAW gunner attachment to 1st Squad, came up to me and asked for the 9 mm he lost and that I'd found at the ambush site. As I handed it back to him, I remembered the men I'd killed with the gun as we cleared houses.

I was physically and mentally exhausted. I lay down on the ground beside our vehicle, my ears still blaring, and slipped deep into thought while looking up at the sky. I replayed the day's events in my head. Nothing seemed real. I replayed every move and every impulse over and over again. A slide show like the one my mother and father used to project onto my bedroom walls clicked inside my head. Flashes of attackers' faces, my rifle, grenades, Tardif's leg, Gardner's face, the terrorist bunker, the room-to-room close-quarter shoot-outs, white ninja-style uniforms, Fedayeen screaming in Arabic, the vials of adrenaline and *khat,* my frontal charge of the bunker, and the body parts—all of these images and sounds ricocheted through my mind.

A grunt trains his whole life for battle. I'd had the privilege of experiencing it now—of playing a tiny role in the War on Terror. I knew guys who went all four years and never got the honor of experiencing combat. They'd reenlist and reenlist just for the chance to contribute—just for the chance to be baptized by fire. And here we were doing it in our first enlistment.

All those times that I'd carried a gun as a teenager had been for shit. My friends at the time and I were prepared to shoot and get shot at over girls, cars, money, or something as stupid as the way someone looked at us. We thought that's what gangsters did, so we did it. But my Marine brothers and I carried weapons to defend our nation against its enemies. We, like the millions who came before us, used the awesome might of America's military power for liberation, not conquest. There's a profound moral difference between the two. Terrorists knowingly and intentionally target civilians, people who never signed up for battle or chose to enter a military conflict. But every ninja-pajama-wearing motherfucker who ambushed us that day had entered that battlefield with the full and complete knowledge of the consequences. When I hear the typical stoner college "genius" blather about how America is "just as evil as the terrorists," I think maybe he or she would do well to remember the distinction. In my past, I've used violence for evil. But I can tell you this much: My brother Marines and I never did.

I looked over at my beloved rifle and ran my shooting hand across the entire length of the weapon. The Rifleman's Creed was right; it made so much sense. I got up to break down and clean my M-16 and M-203. When I broke down my weapon, the smell of carbon wafted past me. I pulled out the bolt. Several slivers of brass were stuck inside. I opened the 203 breach and a shell from a 40 mm round fell out. I remembered that the last round I shot had barely missed the bunker window. 1st Platoon had left a trail of dead terrorists in Al Tarmiya. We weren't sick maniacs. We were Marines. We were the guys who were willing to do the shit that no civilian will do. Nobody who wears the uniform—Marine, sailor, airman, or soldier—does it for the pay. They do it because they love the nation that gives them and their family more than they could ever have dreamed of. People often ask me how my brothers and I did what we did that day. I always say the same thing: "If we didn't do it, who would?" Not everyone can or should wear a uniform. But a person can't expect to live in the best damn country on earth and not be willing to fight and die for it. He or she can't be a freeloader of freedom.

That's something none of the guys I fought with could ever be called. Amazingly, not a single Marine from our squad died that day during the Battle of Al Tarmiya, including Tardif and Gardner. Yet today, Gardner remains paralyzed from the waist down. He has since supported antiwar protest groups speaking out against the president. It's his right to do so. It's a right he's more than earned. But whatever our disagreements about the justness of our mission, I'll never have anything but love and respect for that guy.

As for our squad leader and my friend Tardif, I wondered when I'd see him again. That's the strange thing about the Corps: You spend months or years training and living with total strangers, get slung into the most harrowing experiences of your life together, forge the deepest bonds of brotherhood, and then get ripped apart and dislocated from one another. But the thing is, you never forget them. They stay with you. Always.

10

The Killing Fields

A few days after the Battle of Al Tarmiya, or the "Battle of the Bridge," as we called it, we drove south for hours until we hit As Samawa, about 130 miles southwest of Baghdad. This was to become our new home. This also meant we'd be losing our AAVs. Their time was up and they were going home. Stop loss had now ended and with it each Marine's obligation to stay in beyond his contract. We'd be humping everywhere from now on.

We pulled up to an old Baath Party Headquarters, aka "the Alamo," near a train station that was the headquarters location for RCT-5, which meant no more resupply problems. We unloaded and said our good-byes to our trackers, never to see them again. They were riding all the way to Kuwait, where they would load their tracs on ship and sail home. The company stood outside the wall surrounding the Alamo, where the 82nd Airborne had been living for weeks. The soldiers looked well-fed and well-equipped. We were amazed by their brand-new, top-of-the-line weapons. The only thing they didn't keep in top condition was the Alamo itself, which was a pigsty. Rats crawled through the disheveled and dirty rooms.

Apparently, the soldiers of the 82nd weren't the cleaning freaks that we'd been trained to be.

Ordered to conduct a patrol with the 82nd soldiers, 2nd Squad began loading up on ammo. The soldiers "light-loaded" their gear and assured us nothing would happen. I and the others in 2nd Squad kept our ammo heavy anyhow.

I was expecting a long "foot mobile" into the city of As Samawa. Instead we got on "gators" and drove around the area that surrounded our compound. Gators reminded me of those small motorized carts that zip around at baseball games hauling ice and beer to vending booths. I didn't like riding the gators, because we were one huge target; one well-placed grenade would kill us all. We passed only a few houses and then went to a checkpoint near the compound. There we did a short foot patrol, but only around the immediate area. That's when I asked some soldiers whether they ever went into the city. "Do we look crazy?" they said.

After our patrol and a changeover of the compound, the 82nd got into a fleet of Humvees and headed north, toward the shit. And so now the Marines of Golf Company would play "policemen," something the Army should have continued doing. The Marines are a fighting force, not a stabilizing force. The Corps isn't big enough or funded properly to maintain stability for long periods of time. That's the Army's forte.

With the 82nd gone, word was given to clean out the nasty living spaces. We cleaned out the compound and burned almost everything in sight. In no time, we had the Alamo looking pretty good. The next morning, I took my first shower in a long time. Well, it wasn't really a shower. I just poured water from a bucket over my head, soaped up, and rinsed. That was when I realized how skinny I had gotten. I finished my shower and put on a fresh pair of underwear, socks, and even a clean pair of cammies. The rest of the day was dedicated to resting, fortifying our new home, and preparing to saturate-patrol the city the next day.

That evening I was told I was being nominated for the Navy Cross. I reacted to the news with disbelief. I sincerely didn't believe I had done anything special. I was just getting some in a firefight. That was my job. Besides, there were a helluva lot of guys there with me, each of whom performed with precision and courage. Yet the news of my nomination quickly spread, causing some people to start hating on me and my platoon. The review process for the Navy Cross, second only to the Medal of Honor, would take a year. In the meantime, we had streets to patrol and religious rivalries and tensions to quell.

The city of As Samawa was wracked with lawlessness. People ran weapons and engaged in looting. The city had apparently not been patrolled in a while. The police were still of the Baath Party. First order of business was to establish a solid relationship with the leadership. Egleston spearheaded the effort by building a solid rapport with their police chief (through an interpreter). We told the policemen we would have each squad stop by to say hello every time they were on patrol. In reality, of course, what we were doing was running surveillance and keeping an eye on the former Baath Party members and getting the locals used to seeing our presence. They happily accepted the olive branch of "friendship."

Within weeks, I knew the city like the back of my hand. As we patrolled, mobs of Iraqi children would surround us, singing and chanting, "Yes, yes, mista. Go, go, mista. We love mista." Not exactly Sinatra, but it would do. The kids sang this over and over, singing faster and faster until it started over at a normal pace. If they weren't singing, other children would run up to us with their thumbs up and say, "Good Bush. Good Bush." We would give them a thumbs-up and try to focus on the task at hand. If the crowds or chants got too loud or distracting, the men of the city would shoo the children away for us and smile.

The first patrol we went on was a platoon-sized patrol. We patrolled for several hours and identified some mosques and plotted them on our maps. Many people in the streets were curious to see the Marines. When we got back to the Alamo, it was announced that patrols would be done at the squad level, so that there would always be one squad patrolling the city at all times during the day and two at night. I was a little uneasy about patrolling by squads in a city as large as As Samawa, because if the shit hit the fan, our quick reaction force (QRF) would have a long commute before arriving on the scene for backup. Not to mention that the city was brand new to us. And even though most of the people seemed friendly, I had seen friendly people before in Baghdad—only to then find RPGs on the side of the roads intended to kill us in an ambush.

On my first squad-level patrol, we stuck to the outskirts just outside of town. People came out in hordes. I, and the rest of the squad, felt a little uneasy. The sound of conversations in Arabic filled the air, as did the stench of sewage. There was really no way to distinguish friend from foe. So we would just scan the crowds for weapons. We made our way through dirt fields and neighborhoods with the sun beating on us. We patrolled past a man who was guiding a donkey that had a huge, fly-infested gash in its right front leg. The animal hobbled along with a massive load on its back that caused its wounded leg to buckle periodically. When it did, the man beat the donkey for not walking fast enough. It pissed me off that this jackass (the man, not the animal) was walking his donkey to death. But we were instructed not to interfere with the populace unless it was aggression related. So we patrolled past the man. I never saw the donkey again during my time in As Samawa.

After our three-hour patrol was up, my squad made its way back to the Alamo. My guys dropped their gear and kicked back. I, on the other hand, had to brief the lieutenant. As a fire team leader, I had never put much thought into how a squad leader does so much more than everybody else after missions. But the additional administrative workload now became my routine.

One of the things that broke up the monotony of patrols was mail call. During the invasion, it had been extremely difficult to keep up regular mail delivery to a rifle company like ours that was constantly on the move. But after one long patrol, our company received a large load of mail just before dusk. Staff Sergeant Sikes called out our names. I heard "Martinez" and walked up expecting a letter from my mom and dad (the only people who were writing to me at the time). But when I turned it over, I saw something I didn't want to see—the signature pink writing of the ex-girlfriend I had dumped before leaving for Iraq.

Each Marine took his mail off to a private location and read it. I didn't want to open my letter. But when it was a little darker, I decided to see what she had written. The letter basically said that she was sorry for being selfish and that she wanted me back, something that wasn't going to happen in a million years. Then she started listing things she would do if I didn't get back with her. This was my first "psycho ex-girlfriend letter," a rite of male passage to be sure. I put the letter back in the envelope and walked over to where 1st Platoon had set a fire to brew coffee.

Magana was there, and without saying a word, we exchanged letters. Magana's eyes widened as he read mine. His letter was from a girl he had dated previously. Things hadn't worked out between them, but now suddenly she was all for dating a Marine. We swapped back letters and stared at the flames of the fire. I took one last look at the psycho note and shook my head before tossing it into the fire. Magana did the same. We watched the letters curl and ash before a few other Marines turned the corner, letters in hand, ready to burn their unwanted letters as well.

WE HAD BEEN AT the Alamo for a good four weeks and things were running smoothly. All we needed were vehicles to get to the heart of the city. At this point, we were basically self-sustaining at the Alamo, and, for the most part, we didn't have to put up with any battalion-level bullshit, such as headquarters micromanaging every aspect of patrol schedules and minute details that would irritate the hell out of us. But when a fleet of Humvees pulled up to take us to the train station, our no-bullshit lives came to an end.

Gunny Linton walked around making sure nothing was left behind at the Alamo. "Don't leave nothing for the Hajis!" he yelled.

We set huge fires and burned everything except the buildings. A crowd of Iraqis ("Hajis") stood off in the distance. They knew we were leaving and were chomping at the bit to be the first to see what they could salvage. We loaded in the Humvees and started our drive to the train station. When we looked back down the road, we saw the massive crowd of Hajis running into the Alamo as huge plumes of smoke billowed in the sky.

We traveled three miles east of the Alamo to our new home, which we dubbed "Camp Smitty" in memory of First Sergeant Smith. The train station had five enormous hangar-type buildings and a few smaller buildings attached to it that were occupied by the HQ Marines. The train station's sprawling design made me uneasy. A determined enemy who wanted to infiltrate our living space could do so easily.

We were assigned one of the hangars, which housed numerous train cars. Captain Hammond claimed a train car as his "room" and even somehow acquired a couch to furnish his new home. Egleston and Kelting, both squad leaders, also took a train car, and eventually they got couches too. I opted to sleep on the ground with everybody else. But all of us knew this place would probably be our home until we headed back to the United States, so we spruced it up and even built a few wooden seats and tables.

One way the company made the hangar feel more homey was by dedicating one train car to a fine Cuban woman: Vida Guerra. A whole side of the train car was covered with just about every picture ever taken of Vida, a beautiful Cuban girl who blew up on the scene after posing in *Maxim* magazine. We nicknamed that side of the car the "Vida Guerra motivational wall." The running joke was that if you wondered who or what you were fighting for, you should just go to the wall and look at Vida, because she was worth it.

Over the next several weeks, we would patrol while battling the heat and trying as best we could to build cordial relations with the locals. On one patrol, our corpsman, The Rage, whipped out his thermometer and announced that it was close to 129 degrees. Beyond the heat, though, you had the smell of sewage to deal with. There was no sewage system, so everything was on the ground. You'd roll past empty lots between houses and see "ponds" of human waste. I'll never forget seeing a family of ducks swimming through the disgusting water and wondering how they hadn't died from the toxic sludge.

On patrol, we found an AA gun sandwiched between two buildings at the local elementary school. I radioed our find back to Reaper 6, our CO, who advised me to mark it on the map (no shit). We also rolled to the police station and briefly visited with the police officers. During patrols, we would come in contact with several people who spoke good English. When they would ask our names, we'd give them fake names. What they really wanted more than anything was just to practice saying our names in English.

They'd also ask what state we were from. When Birdsong told them he was from Arkansas, they had no idea what Arkansas was. They knew California, New York, and Texas, but that was about it, just as I'd guess most Americans couldn't name but a handful of Iraqi cities or provinces.

Being at Camp Smitty brought more reminders of the world we had left behind back home—and not always good reminders. It wasn't just psycho ex-girlfriends who were writing. During one mail call, I received a letter from Marine Corps West Credit Union, the bank through which I had financed my car loan and with which I had all my banking accounts. I was shocked to see that even though they knew I was at war (they were located on Camp Pendleton), they had slapped on their own insurance and an additional $4,000 to my loan. I didn't need the extra stress. There in Iraq, the last thing on my mind was my FICO score.

Fortunately, the next letter I opened was from my "California mom," Ginger, who handled my insurance. I called her office, which was in itself a miracle, because back in 2003, it was damn near impossible for a grunt to be granted permission to make a phone call. Ginger got angry when she heard that the bank had dropped a financial bomb on me in the middle of a war. Sure enough, she straightened it all out; a month later, I received a letter of apology from Marine Corps West.

I also received a package from my mom. She sent more religious items, which I put in my breast pocket to carry around with me. No guy will admit it, but getting a letter from your mom adds comfort and brings an extra bit of peace.

When night fell, I inspected my squad for night patrol and made sure each Marine had his NVGs. Evening patrols were less stressful because there were fewer people out on the streets. We left just after dusk. The "Prayer Call" commenced and I quickly had the squad take a security halt and get into positions that could be easily defended. The last thing I wanted was for hostile elements to get any ideas and hit the squad while we were stalled out of respect for their Prayer Call. If the enemy were going to hit us, it would be on our terms.

Just like the one back in Baghdad, the word *jihad* was used in the Prayer Call like a gangster rapper uses the word *fuck*. We all kept an eye out for anybody trying to pull shit. The prayer ended and nothing happened. But soon we would all get a taste of the religious factions and differences that divide Shiite from Sunni when we were tasked with establishing religious contacts with the nine area mosques.

It was going to be a hard job, more diplomacy and policing than anything else. But I had no choice in the matter. To assist me, I was given two interpreters, one Shiite and one Sunni, who had been attached to the company a few days prior. Beyond their religious differences, the two men looked about as opposite as two men could look. The Shiite was thin and had a full head of hair. The Sunni was fat and balding. They were both in their thirties and well-educated and had been teachers in As Samawa. The task I was given was to take a picture with each sheik so that the person being photographed could be identified and so that I could maintain a friendly relationship with each religious leader. The pictures would all be input into a database. Since sheiks run every aspect of their communities, we needed to identify the leadership in the event that these opinion leaders turned against the coalition and began supporting the insurgency (which was in its infancy).

We initially set out with the Sunni interpreter and made the rounds to Sunni mosques. After some initial skepticism, the first sheik befriended me after we offered him a box of MREs. When we snapped the photo, he posed like a model while his congregation watched and clapped. His congregants were amazed to see the picture on the LCD screen of our digital camera. When the sheik asked for a copy of the picture, I told him I would get him one, though I felt a little uncomfortable about having my picture available for all to see.

The sheik at the next mosque was a bit more standoffish. It took all day to build rapport with him and convince him to take a picture with me. As we quickly learned, Iraqi culture has a very different conception of time from our own. Unlike Americans, who are always looking at our watches, the Iraqis didn't stress out over time. And so, when I'd meet with the members of the mosques and their leaders, I'd have to talk with them for over an hour per mosque. It was like going through the formalities of meeting your girlfriend's parents: You just had to do it.

The last Sunni mosque we visited wanted nothing to do with us and the sheik was very abrupt. I tried to befriend him and interact, but to no avail. After a few attempts, we left and plotted the mosque on the map.

The next day, we hit the Shiite mosques with our Shiite interpreter. The Shiites were much friendlier and more welcoming. You still had to go through the same formalities, but it was far more pleasant and cordial. The last mosque we visited that day was among the largest in As Samawa. The sheik was as nice as could be. When I asked him what the name of his mosque was, his reply made me do a double take. "The Martyrs of the Bridge," he said.

He invited us in for tea. I knew the tea could be poisoned, but I also knew that if I refused the sheik, it would be interpreted as a sign of disrespect and could hurt relations. *This one's for the Corps,* I thought to myself. The tea was tasty. After five minutes passed and I hadn't died from poisoning, the rest of the squad drank a cup as well. After endless conversation, we snapped the picture and headed back to the train station, having completed our mission.

ONE DAY AT Camp Smitty, Golf Company's First Sergeant Young, an African American New Yorker with a body like Mike Tyson's, informed me that General Matis wanted to speak to Staff Sergeant Sikes, Lieutenant Maurer, and me about the "Battle of the Bridge." That morning, the three of us stood outside the headquarters command post waiting to speak with the great General Matis. It was obvious he was there, because a CH-46 sat in the empty lot that doubled as a landing zone. After waiting a few minutes, Sergeant Major Davis came out to greet and escort us into the command post. He handed us off to the Battalion Commander, Lieutenant Colonel O'Donohue, who took us into a room in the middle of which stood General Matis. We came to attention. General Matis gave the "at ease" command and all three of us came to a "snap and pop" parade rest position.

"How are you gentlemen?" said General Matis.

In unison we responded, "Outstanding, sir."

"That's good to hear."

The general spoke to Lieutenant Maurer first, since he was an officer. General Matis asked the lieutenant to detail the command and control throughout the Battle of the Bridge. General Matis nodded his head in agreement as Lieutenant Maurer spoke. He'd led and fought in Vietnam and therefore had firsthand experience of being a platoon commander during battle.

Next he spoke to Staff Sergeant Sikes about the actions on the objective performed during the battle. Staff Sergeant Sikes had earned the nickname "Immortal" by crossing gunfire-swept streets before making it to a three-story building—atop which he called in mortars with lethal precision. General Matis seemed pleased with Staff Sergeant Sikes's answers.

I knew my turn was next and didn't want to give another "I like cheeseburgers" answer the way I'd done with the previous general I'd encountered.

"Corporal Martinez, I understand you shot almost every weapon on the battlefield," said General Matis.

I smiled and said, "Almost every weapon, sir."

He laughed and asked me to tell him exactly what I had done and walk him through the sequence of events from start to finish. As I stood there speaking to one of the greatest officers the Marine Corps has seen in a long time, something behind General Matis caught my eye through the window. I tried to stay focused on answering the general's questions and describing the events that had unfolded, but for the life of me I couldn't help but think I was seeing things. The person peering through the window at me looked just like Tardif. The figure started waving at me and making faces, trying to make me lose composure in front of the general. When the guy flipped me a bird, I knew I wasn't seeing things. It was Tardif.

"Is there anything that you would have done differently, Corporal?" asked General Matis.

"No, sir," I said.

He looked at Lieutenant Maurer and Staff Sergeant Sikes and said, "That's what NCOs do—set the pace of the battle." They both agreed. General Matis then put his hand on my shoulder in a fatherly fashion and said, "You have done the Marine Corps and me proud." I thanked him for his gracious words. The general wasn't done, however. He peppered me with questions about the enemy, such as what they wore and how they looked. He was especially interested in their ninja-like suits and the fact that many of the facial features of the men we killed that day led some to believe that they were foreigners, possibly Syrians. We all exchanged pleasantries for a few more moments until Sergeant Major Davis called us to attention. We popped to a sharp position of attention and exited the room.

When we exited the room, Tardif was standing out in front of the command post smoking a cigarette, looking tough as hell. Staff Sergeant Sikes ran up and gave him a hug, lifting the nearly 220-pound Tardif off the ground. Lieutenant Maurer and I likewise gave Tardif hearty hugs and stood before him in awe. When we asked him how the hell he'd gotten here, he told a story of almost being sent home, then convincing a doctor in Ramstein, Germany, to let him go back to Iraq. After convincing the doctor, he caught flight after flight until he found his way to As Samawa. Tardif had given up a chance to go home, something most people would have taken and run with. He'd returned to "get some more," as he put it.

Tardif had no gear except for the Load Bearing Vest (LBV) that he had probably swiped from an "air winger" (someone who works on planes and helos). So I took him to where supply had set up a mobile PX and bought him some socks and other things he needed. As we walked toward the company area, Tardif told me about Ramstein, and how he was glad to be out of such a depressing place. When we got near our company's area, the men of Golf Company bombarded him like a rock star.

But, in traditional Tardif fashion, after greeting everyone, he was eager to get back into the action. As we prepared for patrol, Tardif took off his pants to change his dressings. I looked at him and said, "Holy shit, man! You still have serious wounds!"

"Yeah," he said. "That's why it took so much convincing for the doctor to let me go. They said I hadn't fully healed." But despite the wounds, Tardif went on patrol with the squad.

After the patrol, I asked Lieutenant Maurer what he wanted me to do about our squad leadership position, since Tardif was a senior corporal over me. Later that day, First Sergeant Young summoned me and explained that I would be picking up the rank of sergeant. He said that the higher-ups had decided that my actions during the Battle of the Bridge were enough to make me combat promoted. He instructed me not to tell anyone about our talk. I kept my mouth shut as ordered.

Days later, a promotion ceremony was held in a building dubbed "Club Chaos," which was a recreation room with an air conditioner. Had there not been an air conditioner, the guys forced to attend my promotion ceremony would have likely killed me. A company formation was called just like back in the States. After my citation was read aloud, the battalion commander asked me whom I wanted to pin me. I asked for Staff Sergeant Sikes and Corporal Tardif, who both came up and pinned on my rank. After that, the company was dismissed and Staff Sergeant Sikes stopped me and congratulated me once again. He then looked around to make sure nobody was looking and slammed the bottom of his fist onto the rank on my collar. I guess some traditions never die.

THREE OTHER THINGS served as pick-me-ups during our final months in Iraq. The first of these was the Seabees unit that got attached to our camp. The Seabees, a unit of older men hailing from New York, built showers, tables, chairs, and everything else you could think of. They even set up a little barbershop in an old storage room. It was like being back home, since the barber knew your name and would shoot the shit with you while he cut your hair. The walls of the barbershop were covered with pinup girls from magazines like *Maxim* and *FHM*. Right in front of the chair hung good ol' Vida Guerra. God Bless America!

When the Seabees completed the showers, we all thought we'd died and gone to heaven. I took showers every day, sometimes two or three times a day. People started to make fun of me and call me "Mr. Clean." But hey, I'm a clean freak, and if showers were there, I was going to take advantage.

The second boost to morale came a few weeks later when we were visited by "Gunny" R. Lee Ermey, a Marine who served in Vietnam who's best known for playing the drill instructor in the movie *Full Metal Jacket.* When he arrived, he was in full character, pretending to be Gunny Hartman from the movie. He delivered all his famous lines from *Full Metal Jacket,* which we all knew by heart, and we replied "Sir, yes, sir!" at the appropriate times. When he broke character, he told us that back home our country supported us and for all the rest to go fuck themselves. Needless to say, we loved the guy. He visited with us and snapped pictures and was kind and gracious with his time.

The final thing that helped break up the monotony between patrols was that some kids from a high school in Keyes, California, wrote us to show their support. I received a letter addressed to "Any Marine" from a girl named Synae Ferrer. It was genuine and thoughtful, so I wrote her back, beginning a correspondence that lasted my last couple of months in Iraq and continues to this day. It meant a lot that a total stranger—a high school student, no less—would take the time to write a grunt like me.

I received another letter addressed to "Any Troop." But this couldn't have been more different from Synae's. This one was from a girl who went on and on about why she thought the war was wrong. She made it a point to say she was an AP high school student. She was obviously an expert military strategist and political Einstein who thought she would get the last laugh. Instead, I got a piece of paper and a Sharpie and wrote her my own special letter:

FUCK YOU, BITCH
USMC

I sealed it with a kiss (hocked a big loogie), folded it neatly, and put it inside an envelope before dropping it in the outgoing mail sack.

Isn't freedom of speech great?

A FEW WEEKS LATER, Tardif and I were ordered to report to Captain Hammond. Tardif had been nominated for a Silver Star. We were told that ABC News wanted to interview us about the Battle of the Bridge and that we'd be joining some of the Marines from Fox Company for a trip to Kuwait City for media interviews. I had met and been interviewed by reporter Mike Cerre at the outset of the war. Now he had asked Tardif and me to appear on film and recount our stories. Mike was a helluva guy and a former Marine lieutenant who had fought in Vietnam. Unlike most of the smart-ass reporters who were barely older than us and thought they had it all figured out, Mike treated us with respect and understood the shit we were going through.

ABC News put us up in a Hilton, the nicest hotel I've ever seen in my life. It might as well have been a palace. The thing that was so strange about being in Kuwait was that life was going on just like normal. Businesses hummed, men with multiple wives (gorgeous wives, I might add) walked through the city, and restaurants and shop owners smiled and went about their work as usual. The idea that there was a war taking place just across the border didn't even seem to be on their radar screens. When Tardif and I were in the hotel lobby, we were amazed to see a group of Kuwaiti high school students all decked out in prom gear and getting ready for their big night out on the town.

Shortly after we got back from our trip to Kuwait, Captain Hammond announced that there would be a change of command and that Captain Kenny would be taking his place. Captain Kenny was a large man and came straight from Officer's Infantry Course (OIC). He had been an instructor for the school of infantry for officers and had even instructed Lieutenant Maurer when he was going through. Usually when there is a change of command, it is for the worst, because the new commander is fresh and wants to show how hard he is and to "set the pace." But Captain Kenny was smart. He understood that a war zone was no place to start slinging one's weight around.

His focus was on building relational bridges among the religious leaders in the city. He knew that I'd previously been tasked with making religious contacts and so he asked me to join him in visiting with some of the local sheiks. One of those we visited was the sheik at the Martyrs of the Bridge mosque, with whom I had previously had cordial and warm interactions. This time the sheik met us with the same friendliness as he had before, but something seemed a little off. As we made our way through the mosque compound, we were told there were certain "praying houses" we weren't allowed to enter. But when a Marine walked through a side hallway and passed by a door that had been left ajar, he saw a huge bottle of nitroglycerin and some other bomb-making materials. We informed Captain Kenny, who later planned and executed a raid on the building. Sure enough, the Marines seized bomb-making materials there. It was another reminder of the deep divisions pervasive in Iraq. You often didn't know a friend from a foe.

But despite all the complicated political aspects and entanglements, one thing more than anything else made me certain that our mission was and remains just: seeing and guarding the mass graves. When we were tasked with guarding the mass graves located near the small town of Solman, I learned that the graves contained thousands of decayed corpses and skeletons. We were in the middle of nowhere; were we to be attacked, it would have been hours before reinforcements could arrive. We would rotate on four-day shifts and take seven-ton trucks with escorts to get there.

When we arrived, we set up the best perimeter we could. The area looked like something you would see in a movie where some poor soul roams the desert in desperate search of water and dies. Setting up our defense, we had to pass three burial sites. The graves were massive craters in the ground. I stopped to look at one and immediately saw numerous human skeletal remains, such as skulls with holes punched through the tops of them. I shook my head and thought of the dumbasses who said that the people of Iraq were better off under Saddam. Ironically, these are the same people who are always first in line to decry human rights abuses. But then, when we try and do something about such abuses, they don't want to get their hands dirty and actually have to "fight" for others' freedom. I'd like those people to see the mass graves in Iraq and the bodies of the thousands of people Saddam exterminated and then tell me again how great life was under Saddam.

As we surveyed the graves, locals recounted what we already knew: Saddam ordered his army to gather up Kuwaitis during the first Gulf War and Iraqis who opposed Saddam's regime and drive them out into the middle of nowhere (where we stood). Once there, Saddam's henchmen tied two people together, some with babies in their arms, stood them at the crater's edge and shot one of the two people in the head, relying on the weight of the dead body to drag them both down into the hole. This would save on rounds and also ensure that both people died, one from a gunshot, the other by being buried alive.

The craters looked as though somebody had tried to move the

remains but had given up. We stayed in the harsh landscape for four days at a time and pulled this duty many times over. But instead of being numbed by the repeated trips to the graves, each time I grew more sickened and haunted by the thoughts of what had happened to the people who lay under the earth in front of me. The graves were so high profile that U.S. government agents came out to survey the graves. But for me, staring into those massive holes and seeing the bones and skulls was all the evidence I needed. For me, those graves were proof positive that the "weapon of mass destruction" wasn't some chemical-tipped missile, but Saddam Hussein himself.

MY TOUR WAS winding down to a close when the Fourth of July rolled around. The battalion had set up a hot dog and hamburger BBQ and provided a soda for each man. My feast was short-lived, though, because I had a patrol scheduled that night. Because of this, my squad was allowed to go to the front of the line and was given a good twenty minutes to chow down and drink our sodas before heading off to patrol. But to tell you the truth, I think that was one of the best Fourth of July celebrations I've ever been a part of. I was with my squad and was doing what I'd dreamed of doing since I was a boy. During our dusk patrol, many shots rang out, something not unusual in Iraq. Iraqis shot guns in the air for everything that made them happy. Life didn't stop just because there was a war going on in their country. People still got married (gunshot) and had babies (gunshot) and celebrated birthdays (gunshot). Life went on.

One night, I happened to be on SOG (sergeant of the guard) along with a staff sergeant from HQ who was reading the book *Jarhead.* He started mumbling out about how awful the book was. He was a little less than halfway through, but suddenly he threw the book down in a huff.

"Damn, this book is full of shit!" said the staff sergeant.

Startled, I asked, "Can I see it?"

He picked the book up and handed it to me, but he warned me, "All this guy does is bitch about how terrible the Marine Corps is!"

The pissed-off staff sergeant left. I started reading the book to see what had fired him up so much. By the time I was relieved from my post, I had read enough not to like the book. In fact, I hated it. I walked back to the company area and headed for the shitters. They were little more than boxes with a hole cut out for a seat, under which were placed huge metal drums that had been cut in half to catch the waste. Each morning and night, some unfortunate Marine would have to pour diesel fuel in the drums and light the waste on fire while stirring the burning fecal stew. Terrone, Mr. Frank Sinatra, had been the poor soul who had to burn the shit that day. I took a leak in the "piss tubes" and walked over to one of the burning drums and threw the book into one of the flaming shit soufflés.

"Why are you burning that book?" said Terrone.

"You'd have to read it to understand," I said.

THE SAME DAILY schedules continued. Patrols lasted all day or all night. We guarded the local hospital against thieves and protected its patients against militants who may try to kill them. Via the World Food Program, we fed the city's population, including former Iraqi Army soldiers who more than likely had fought against U.S. troops during the invasion. Mass-grave security continued as well, as did joint patrols with the Iraqi police to maintain the peace in As Samawa.

Then, in August, we got word that we were next to rotate back to the United States. When we made the long drive to Kuwait and got near the Iraq-Kuwait border, I wondered whether I'd ever see this place or experience war again. But somehow I already knew the answer.

Our vehicles rolled across the border, and just like that, I was no longer in a war zone. We were told to unload our weapons but to keep them slung. My tour in Iraq had ended. I was a garrison Marine again.

11

Rifle Sight Is 20/20

Coming home, our first stateside stop was Bangor, Maine. It felt good to be back in America. Walking down a long airport corridor, we noticed that a large crowd of people had gathered at the terminal gate. We shot one another confused looks. Most of us figured the people were hippie protestors. We were ready to fight if needed. But as we got closer and closer, we realized they weren't protestors at all. They were some of the most wonderful people we'd ever met. They were the "troop greeters of Bangor, Maine."

More than a hundred people, most of them slow and gray, held signs and cheered and applauded for us as we stepped out into the terminal. Little old ladies, Boy Scouts, and veterans from wars fought long ago hugged us and patted us on the back. "Welcome home!" they said. "We support you. Thank you!" A Vietnam veteran walked up to me and hugged me.

"Never be ashamed of your service," he said.

"I can't be ashamed, sir, because we did it for America," I replied.

His eyes began to water. The old warrior handed me a cell phone and told me to call my parents, who were probably worried about me. I called my mom and talked to her for a few minutes before passing the phone to another Marine.

When I looked around, I saw my friends sharing similar moments with the wonderful troop greeters who had taken time out of their lives to wait for a plane full of Marines, none of whom they knew, just to say thank you. I watched the Vietnam veterans. I could tell they were happy to give us something they'd been robbed of: a warm and respectful homecoming. We talked with all the people who had gathered and thanked them for everything they had done. When our time was up, I looked back over my shoulder one final time at the vets proudly wearing their embroidered hats and ribbons and could tell that they saw themselves in us.

We arrived at March Air Force Base in California to no crowd and boarded the buses back to Camp Pendleton. On the way, some people gave us a thumbs-up. Others flipped us off. When we got to Pendleton, only family and friends of Marines and sailors were there. They waved flags and support signs and waited to unite with their loved ones.

We turned in our weapons to the armory and were put on a "96," which is ninety-six hours off, or a four-day extended weekend. Magana's cousins picked us up and took us to a family barbecue in Santa Ana. As relaxing as it was to eat some barbecue and drink a Corona with Magana in the backyard, I realized that being home would take some getting used to. After we ate, I felt like I had to go on patrol. But that was over now. I didn't have to "scan" the backyard. I could eat "dinner," not "chow." To this day I'm still getting used to it all.

Some of Magana's high-school-age cousins asked us questions about Iraq. They were taken aback by our bluntness about how it really was. We didn't sugarcoat anything and used graphic details—

the mass graves, the tortured Iraqis, etc.—that challenged the spin they were hearing from the media.

The next day, Magana and I bought the Rolexes we'd joked about and used as motivators to make it through the war.

Soon it was time for me to return home to my own family. Catching a flight from San Diego to El Paso, I sat by myself in the back of the plane so I could see everything that was happening. I drank a Coke and tried to relax, but couldn't. When the plane touched down, I tried to make myself look happy for my mom. I got up and said to myself, "Okay, here we go!"

I walked down the lobby and spotted my parents and smiled. I expected my mom to run up and make a big deal the way she had when I stepped into this very terminal after boot camp. But she didn't (thanks, Mom). She knew I hated that type of thing. No, instead she was very reserved and kept looking at me like I was an impostor. I felt a little uncomfortable. I hugged them both and they expressed how glad they were that I was home. As we walked out of the terminal, I noticed several armed soldiers with M-16s walking around in post–September 11 America. *It's about time,* I thought.

We got into my dad's truck and headed home. I showed my parents my Rolex. They were glad I was enjoying my war money. But the ride home was awkward and mostly silent. Driving the forty-five-minute stretch of desert terrain from El Paso to Las Cruces, I kept taking mental notes about possible ambush sites along the highway. We pulled into the driveway and I saw both my '99 Camaro and my '86 Monte Carlo sitting there. I couldn't wait to drive. But that would be for later.

Inside the house I greeted my triplet sisters and we sat down to eat the feast my mother had prepared for my homecoming. I started to relax a bit more and talk with my parents about things unrelated to Iraq. I flicked on the television, but soon became so disgusted at the biased news coverage of the war in Iraq that I turned off the TV and went to my room. My mother came in to check on me, and though I told her I was fine, I could tell she was worried about me. A short while after she left, my dad entered my room. I told him that the knife he had bought me came in handy and thanked him again for buying it. Sensing that I wanted some time to myself, my father left the room. I got up and changed into some running gear, surprising my mom. Where was I going so late? she wondered. I said I was going for a run.

I took off running into the darkness at a fast pace. I ran the same route I had taken the night I walked home from high school graduation. I started to run faster. I ran past the Aggie Car Wash and then took a left past a plaza. Keeping up the same pace, I passed the Dairy Queen and crossed the street onto the same running path I'd run with my friend Tony Morales. I ran faster, remembering the spot where a group of high school friends had yelled "loser" at me because I was going into the Marines. I kept going. I didn't stop. I sped up. I ran miles and miles before finally getting winded and turning home. I was drenched in sweat but controlled my breathing.

After a sleepless night, the next day I hung out with some friends. But it wasn't the same. They asked questions about Iraq, and I tried to be as patient as possible, but I blew up when one started in with the ignorant antiwar comments typical among civilian teens and twenty-somethings.

That kind of experience, I soon learned, wouldn't be unusual back in the States. They'd seen a Michael Moore movie. We'd seen the mass graves. People seemed compelled to tell me their views on the war even though I never asked for any thoughts on the subject. Several weeks after our leave ended, the city of Oceanside, California, held a welcome-home parade for us. The majority of those who came out that day were supportive and gracious. But toward the end of the parade, a group of antimilitary types and war protestors gathered to throw things in our direction, shout obscenities, and even spit on the ground as we passed by. They yelled foul things about us, the Marine Corps, and the military in general.

OUR LAST MONTHS at Camp Pendleton were spent training. Our boots received boots of their own; things had come full circle. Many of us contemplated reenlisting but also wanted to see what the civilian world offered. For months I wrestled with the decision. It tore me apart. To help me make my decision, I shadowed SOI instructors to see how the new system was running. While I was there, I saw Sergeant Waters—who was now *Staff* Sergeant Waters. He was teaching a land navigation class to a bunch of new students. I wanted to go up to him and talk, but I didn't want to interrupt him. Even after his class was over, I couldn't push myself to thank him for being such a tremendous instructor. It was because of him that I learned never to do anything at less than 110 percent. But I didn't thank him for teaching me how to go savage and become a wrecking ball during combat. So let me muster the courage now: Thank you, Staff Sergeant.

In December 2003, I went on recruiter's assistance, which is somewhat rare for a sergeant to do. But I wanted to see how things worked. I knew I was not cut out to be a recruiter when one of the sergeants of the office and I visited Mayfield High School during lunch. We set up a table and many kids passed by, scared to talk to us. Recruiters have to make the first move most of the time. So we each struck up conversations with different kids about the possibility of making the Marine Corps their career. The students' interest ranged from not interested at all to mildly interested. Some kids said their reason for not joining was that their parents wouldn't approve.

But one kid in particular really pissed me off, thus proving I wasn't cut out to be a recruiter. I walked up to him and started a conversation. He was a young punk who thought he was a gangster. He had the persona down pat and fronted like he was a straight-up gangster.

"Hey, bro. What grade are you in?" I asked.

"Twelfth," he said.

"What are your plans after high school?"

"I got a job at Burger King. I'm going to fix up my car."

"Don't you want to get out of this place?"

"Like where?"

"California."

"Really?"

"Yeah. The Marine Corps has a lot of things to offer. Look, man. I got a Rolex, a nice car"—I pointed to my Monte Carlo— "and you could get out of this place and see the world, bro."

"Would I have to go to war?"

"There is always that possibility. But that's what the military is there for. Don't you want to serve your country? I went to Iraq and here I am."

"Naw, man. I don't want to go to war."

And this is about when I realized I wasn't exactly "recruiter material."

I got pissed.

"I thought you were a straight-up gangster, homeboy. You're just a fucking pussy."

The kid looked at me like he wanted to fight.

"What the fuck you going to do? I'll fuck you up in a quick second. You ain't no gangster. Get the fuck out of my face."

He tried to save face. "Well, do I *have* to go to war?"

"What the fuck kind of question is that?" I snapped back.

The wannabe gangster walked off feeling low. The sergeant I was with got a little mad at me for my unconventional sales pitch but said he understood where I was coming from.

After that, I was not allowed to go on any more school visits.

After my recruiter experience, I knew there was no place for me in the Marines except the grunts. Infantry was where I belonged. A guy is either born a grunt or born a POG. I was a grunt and was damn proud of it.

I considered going back to Iraq with Golf Company, but I knew the ROEs were getting way too strict for us to complete the mission and do what was needed to be done. From what I heard and saw, the United States was increasingly tying the troops' hands behind their backs on the front lines of a war in which we were fighting savage killers. After much thought and deep soul-searching, I decided to get out.

ON MAY 3, 2004, I was summoned to Camp Pendleton in San Mateo, home of the 5th Marines, to receive the Navy Cross. In the same ceremony, Tardif and Staff Sergeant Sikes received Silver Stars. I stood there at the position of attention as a Navy Cross was pinned on my chest. In front of me was Secretary of the Navy Gordon England, to whom I snapped off a sharp salute. He smiled and thanked me for honorable service. Media were in full force. Every few seconds, I heard the clicks of cameras. Lieutenant Colonel O'Donohue and Sergeant Major Davis stood proudly behind England. I could see my mother in the background beaming with pride.

But where were the Marines who had gotten me there? Where were my brothers—all of 2/5—who'd risked their lives just as much as I had in Iraq? Where were the men who'd trained us and made us

Marines and men? Where were men like the legendary First Sergeant Bell or Staff Sergeant Waters? I was a repentant shithead who'd been privileged enough to get numerous second chances, and I was humbled to have been given the opportunity to become a United States Marine. I was no more a hero than anyone else who served with honor. But I was the one receiving the medal.

They read my citation and the words took me back to the day when one of the most surly rifle platoons in 5th Marines got some in a major way. We fought and bled for one another. And as the Bible says, there's no greater love than that of a man who would lay down his life for a friend.

After the ceremony, Marines of all ranks, both enlisted and officers, came to talk to me. Everyone was too gracious and kind, and all the focus and attention made me more than a little uncomfortable. After several newspaper and television interviews, my old platoon mates found me and congratulated me. These were the same guys who had once been my boots and were now themselves leading men. The torch had been passed. It felt good. They made me proud.

After I spoke with Lieutenant Maurer, who was awarded the Bronze Star with a *V* for Valor weeks earlier, and Miguel, a representative from the Legion of Valor approached me and inducted me as a lifetime member. And just like that, I was a civilian again.

Because I was already on terminal leave when I received the Navy Cross, it never graced my uniform. Given my past, this, I think, was poetic justice. But deep in my heart, both then and now, I knew I'd been transformed, that the kid who'd tried desperately to belong and be hard was long gone.

AFTER THE CORPS, I moved to Florida for a brief stint and then back to California, where I live now. Today I'm twenty-six years old and work full-time guarding government facilities while also going to college to get my degree in business. Sometimes professors or students start in about the War on Terror and Iraq. One student who was appalled that I was a Marine told me, "You're a disgusting human being, and I hope you rot in hell!" But when I hear things like that, I try to keep my mouth shut. I don't blame them. They don't know any better. They just parrot what they read online or watch on TV. If you've ever served, you know just what I mean. Even if we explained everything, they'd still never understand.

One person who did understand was my father, a former Army Ranger. I use the past tense because my father died during the writing of this book. He never got to read the manuscript. But you know what? He didn't need to. He lived it too. The more I meditate on his untimely and unexpected passing, the more I realize how so much of my life has been a quest to be worthy of being his only son. He never put that onus on me; I did. But I'm grateful that God gave me a father of honor and strength, one whose passion for family and America drove the choices he made. Just as he had wanted it, he died an American citizen, a privilege he earned through a career in the United States Army. My father died well before his time. But he understood.

Yet not everyone was meant to understand what it takes to keep a nation free. Not everyone was meant to understand hardcore devotion to military service, or to our beloved Corps. Not everyone was meant to value a brother's life as much as you value your own.

But that's okay. That's as it should be.

Not everyone was meant to be Hard Corps.

Epilogue

Parting Shots

THEY SAY THAT those who experience combat never see the world the same way again. That's been true for me. I've seen the world through rifle sights. Everywhere I go, the war is present. When I get stuck in traffic, it reminds me of Baghdad. When I'm on my college campus, it reminds me of an open-air market in Iraq. And I just can't shake it.

But here's the thing: I wouldn't trade my time in the Corps or in Iraq for anything in this world.

Each day, I fill my lungs with California ocean air as if God told me it was going to be my last. I appreciate that I survived a war in which others died. I grieve over their deaths and thank God that such men lived and that their actions saved lives.

Before I joined the Corps, I never cared, or even realized, how precious life truly was or how much I had to be thankful for. But now I do. Even my *food* tastes different. The reason for all of this is simple: As a shithead, I was ready to die, but now I'm ready to live. You'll never know how precious God's gift of life is until somebody has threatened to take it from you.

When I drive my car and listen to the music we listened to in Iraq, I can see the faces of my platoon mates. They are dirty and tired, but they are still joking, still laughing, and still talking shit.

Still, I can't seem to watch TV without being reminded that my brothers continue to die on foreign soil. I, like millions of people, pray for them and their families. I hope we never stop praying.

There's another reason I can't ever forget Iraq. I brought a piece of it home with me. My ears never stop ringing. Others left limbs and lives on the battlefield; loud blaring in one's ears is a tiny price to pay. But the sound serves as a helpful twenty-four-hour-a-day reminder that the War on Terror continues; the ringing not likely to cease during my lifetime.

There are no shortcuts. The heavy lifting of history is never easy and seldom desirable.

So the troops do what the millions of Marines, soldiers, sailors, and airmen before us did: We prepare for war and pray for peace. And in between, we honor the dead by living lives filled with laughter and love. Because they died for us, we'll live for them.

Somehow, every generation of Americans before us found a way through.

We will, too.

Acknowledgments

FIRST AND FOREMOST, I would like to thank God, because without Him, I would never have gotten this far in life. God was there when nobody else was. There were plenty of times in my life when I could have died. But You chose to keep me alive. I'm eternally grateful. Thank You.

I wish to thank my parents. I continuously put you through hell, but you never stopped loving or supporting me. You are the definition of unconditional love. You mean more to me than I know how to express.

I'd like to thank Joe and Mary Trejo for being there for my family since I was a small boy and for writing me while I was in Iraq.

I wish to extend my thanks to Richard Lukens for a lifelong friendship and for keeping my family informed while I was in Iraq.

I extend my appreciation and love to each and every member of 1st Platoon and our attachments. Thank you for allowing me to serve alongside you and to be a part of the best platoon any rifleman could dream of being in. Brothers for life.

Two of those guys, Michael Egleston and Carlos Magana, were kind enough to share their memories of our experiences together and remind me of things I'd forgotten. I'm grateful for their time and generosity.

I want the Seabees to know how much I appreciated their making life bearable while 2/5 was stationed at Camp Smitty 2003. Thank you for all you guys do.

Synae Ferrer took time out of her high school experience to faithfully write me all those letters while I was in Iraq. Thank you. The world is yours.

In Iraq—and throughout my life—music has been a huge source of encouragement and motivation. A special thanks to the following: Frost, SPM, A Lighter Shade of Brown, Latino Velvet, NB Ridaz, Knight Owl, Slow Pain, Lil' Rob, Psycho Realm, Cypress Hill, 2Pac, Dr. Dre, Snoop Dogg, Xzibit, Westside Connection, DPG, Brotha Lynch Hung, Spice 1, Bone Thugs-n-Harmony, Ja Rule, Murder Inc, Blackstreet, Keith Sweat, Rome, and Mariah Carey. For holding me down with all the jams and taking me back while I was at war, I thank you. Also, I would like to thank Kid Rock and Korn. And on behalf of my brother grunts, I want to thank Drowning Pool for their song "Bodies," the unofficial Marine Corps anthem.

I also extend my sincere appreciation to Vida Guerra. Thank you for motivating an entire company of grunts through your pictures.

I'm exceedingly grateful to my editor, Jed Donahue, and everyone at Crown Forum who believed in this project from the start and devoted their time and expertise to bringing my book to fruition. Likewise, I am grateful for my literary agent, Joe Vallely. As a Vietnam veteran himself, Joe understood and was passionate about *Hard Corps* from the start. Thank you, Joe, for your service both to me and to our nation.

I'm grateful to Mr. Steve Forbes for showing me New York from Park Avenue. Thank you for your kindness and class.

Wynton Hall: Without you, this book would have never been possible. Words cannot express my appreciation and gratitude for your efforts and friendship throughout the writing of this book. You are truly the consummate professional.

I thank the Barbadillo family for allowing me to stay and work in their San Diego home during the final phase of this book.

Finally, I wish to thank Christine Barbadillo. Never have you passed judgment on me, and never have you been unwilling to help me balance school and work while writing this book. For that, and much more, I remain grateful.